# OREGON PRIZEFIGHTERS

*Forgotten Bare-Knuckle Champions of Portland & Astoria*

BARNEY BLALOCK

THE History PRESS

Published by The History Press
Charleston, SC
www.historypress.net



First published 2015

Manufactured in the United States

ISBN 978.1.62619.993.4

Library of Congress Control Number: 2015943184

*For my godson Mike*

# Contents

Preface 7
Introduction. From the London Fancy to the Oregon Frontier 11

1. The Moonlight Excursion, Being a Narrative Based on Several Reports 21
2. The Fistic Fever Sets In 31
3. A Dogfight with Frenchmen 38
4. The "Nonpareil" 43
5. Near the Mouth of the Lewis River 57
6. 1886: A Year with No Equal 62
7. The Wild Boys of Astoria 83
8. The Unfamiliar Taste of Defeat 88
9. The Pastime at the Cyclorama 98
10. Portland's Mysterioso 117

Afterword. Three Portland Champions for the Ages 137
"Jack Dempsey's Grave" (Poem) 147
Notes 149
Index 155
About the Author 159

# Preface

While researching the underworld of the Portland waterfront for my previous books, I became fascinated by Portland's connection with the prizefighting craze that had spread to the Northwest by the mid-1880s. During the early years of this craze, north end saloons could be found with regulation prizefighting rings in use. "Old Joe Taylor's place" at 135 Front Avenue (old address system) is an example. Taylor was the promoter who first brought Jack "Nonpareil" Dempsey to town to fight a young upstart, a volunteer fireman named Dave Campbell. Because the sport was against the law, anyone connected with prizefighting events was subject to fines and imprisonment. The champions, however, became heroes in many eyes, including those of lawmen, judges and even Theodore Roosevelt, who spoke of heavyweight champion John L. Sullivan in these words:

> *Old John L. has been a greater power for good in this country than many a highly respectable person who would scorn to meet him on terms of equality. He has been my friend many years, and I am proud to be his.*

The central figures of this book are the champion prizefighters who chose Portland as their home. Foremost among them were Dave Campbell, Jack "Nonpareil" Dempsey and "Mysterious" Billy Smith. These were bold and fearless men who were not afraid to go against the strongest opponents of the day. The stories of their lives as Portlanders are a fascinating part of local history that has been overlooked—shuffled into oblivion by turn-of-the-century reformers, prohibitionists and the "progressives" of the day. These reformers saw drunkenness, prizefighting and anything else that offended a sort of deist puritan morality as part of a dark age that was coming to an end, legislated away by a wave of enlightened public opinion. Thus, many

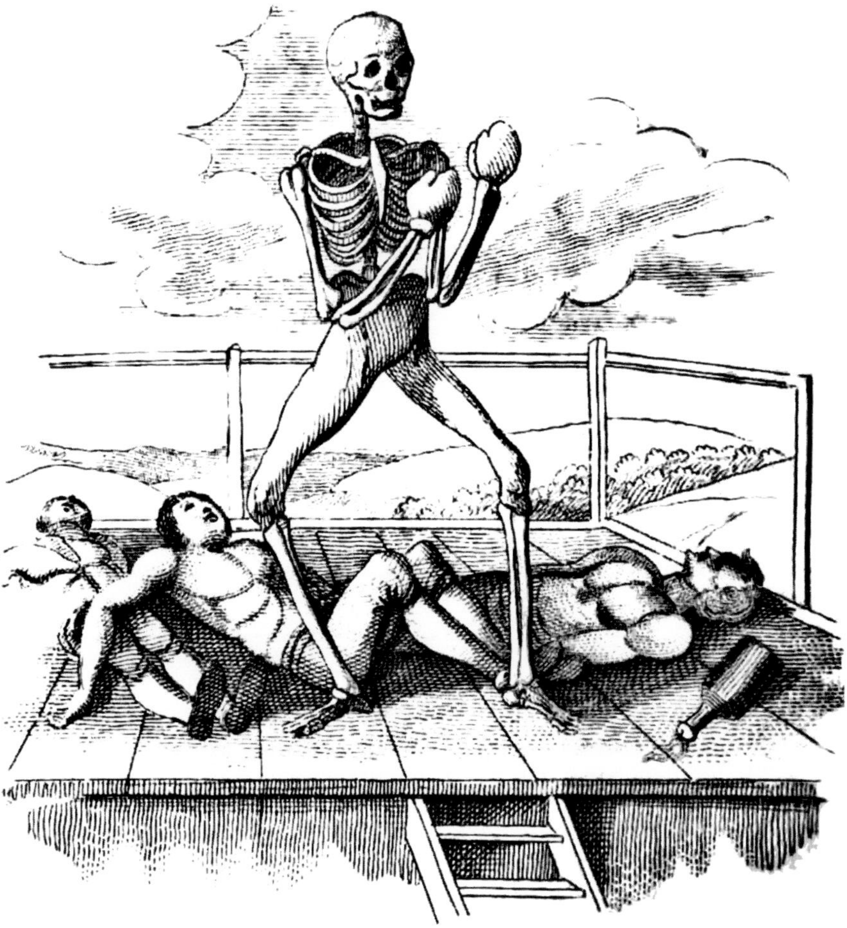

THE CHAMPION.

"The Champion," R. Dagley. *From Charles Ewer*, Death's Doings, *Boston, 1828.*

of the tales of Portland's sordid past died out during seventeen long years of prohibition (three years longer in Oregon than nationally).

The "lower classes" did not leave behind glowing biographies of one another as did the bankers, politicians and judges of the day. The only records remaining are public ones—police reports, newspaper articles, city directories and census reports. In the 1930s, the old stories were supplanted by a new breed of stories, mostly attributable to writer Stewart Holbrook. Those tales, as entertaining as they may be, took the place of a forgotten history. Fortunately, the old world still exists, in all its starkness and unfamiliarity, in the pages of the old newspapers carefully preserved for us by those thoughtful archivists and librarians for whose labors I am very grateful. I am also happy to find that there is a new breed of Portlander, young and old alike, who is not content with invented folklore but is satisfied only by a local history that exudes those unmistakable and intoxicating vapors of a reality that is past.

I would like to thank my daughter, Molly Gunderson (librarian), for her help in tracking down valuable material. I also thank the kind librarian at Tulane University who scanned rare and valuable material for my use. I thank Scott Rook and all of the helpful staff at the Oregon Historical Society for their assistance with images. I am also thankful to my editors at The History Press, Jaime Muehl and Candice Lawrence, who worked hard to make this book a success. I find that I am forever grateful to all the library workers around the world who—in this digital age—spend monotonous hours scanning and compiling online databases. Present and future generations of researchers salute you. Finally, I thank my wife, whose sharp eye and quick wit are just what my manuscripts need—without her I would be lost.

*Introduction*

# From the London Fancy to the Oregon Frontier

Two fists—the most basic of weapons—have been used throughout history by nearly everyone at one time in their lives. In every corner of the world, the pummeling has gone on, with no sign of letting up. From the schoolyard to the neighborhood tavern, impromptu battles are fought in anger, while on television sets around the world professionals duke it out for supremacy. During the time of the Great Enlightenment in Britain, the idea of science and using scientific methods was on the rise, filling every facet of life. Soon, there rose a "fistic science" that liberated the blood sport of pugilism—as it was practiced by bullies in the villages and slums—to that of a "science" that could be equally practiced by gentlemen and ruffians alike.

This new science of slugging gave rise to a cast of characters made up from every class and race of the Empire. This brotherhood of pugilists came to be called—for reasons known only to long-dead Brits—"the Fancy."

In those years following the Slavery Abolition Act of 1833, the English were in the habit of demonizing Americans for the continued practice of slavery, while the Americans demonized the British for, among other things, their love of the brutal sport of prizefighting. In a humorous travelogue, American David Ross Locke wrote:

> *The low Londoner has very brutal tastes. His greatest delight is a prize fight…Gathered around the arena will be a hundred or more of "the fancy," who were to me anything but fancy. They are the broad-jawed, soap-locked, sturdy brutes, of the Bill Sykes type, beer-bloated and gin-*

> *inflamed, who subsist by practices which, if not absolutely criminal, come as close to it as possible.*

It is apparent from an item in an 1860 edition of *Punch* (the foremost British humor magazine) that this term, "the Fancy," was in such common usage at the time that the author of the *Punch* article supposed the only sort of person not using the term was some sheltered, "innocent" lady whom he invited, "if she is pretty," to visit his office, where it would be explained. The joke of the article had to do with the irony that the "the Fancy" was setting the rules of male fashion for "whiskas" and other "facial decoration." The smoothly shaved faces of the young gentry were being replaced by the muttonchops and mustachios of the bare-chested gladiators famous for beating out one another's brains. It would be even more ironic if the fashion of bizarre facial hair worn by men around the world throughout the nineteenth century originated with the pomp and bravado of the prize ring.

Fancy they were, though! Strutting aristocrats wearing gorgeous robes to cover their near nakedness. Burly blacksmiths, cobblers and peasants, the burliest and most powerful rising to challenge the other "scientists" of the ring with loud and obnoxious threats. The ebony muscles of African gladiators could be seen among them, men with the power of two fists to prove their worth. To separate themselves from the riffraff, some of them donned spangled robes and wore crowns of sparkling metal.

The Fives Court in London—where could be found the ring and the Fancy—was one of the most homogeneous regions on God's earth. Even the crowds who thronged the prizefights were utterly homogenous: every form of tradesman, publican, shopkeeper and laborer—some with their women—was in attendance, and scattered among them were various members of the gentry, barristers and clergy mixed in with pickpockets and prostitutes. The most sought-after individual at a prizefight, though, was the bookmaker.

Yet all of this was against the law (according to interpretation, I suppose). The laws already in force were enough. The Riot Act of 1715 called for the arrest of anyone involved in a gathering of just twelve people "unlawfully, riotously and tumultuously assembled together, to the disturbance of the publick peace." It wasn't a far stretch to use that act against prizefights. Then there was illegal bet making—the latter being the grease that oiled the Fancy machine. Some folks will beat another man senseless just for the sport, but most need a reason. So there were fat prizes for the fighters and money to be made by the wheelbarrow load by the bookmakers (and the pickpockets).

# INTRODUCTION

King George the IV was reported to be fond of prizefighting, so as one can imagine, it was sometimes difficult to enforce laws that the king and lords ignored. It is also reported in some books of the period that it was not uncommon for a young gentleman of high birth to gamble away a fortune at the prize ring and then turn to the vocation of highwayman to restore some of the treasure.

Before the end of the eighteenth century, this "fancy" fad had become a craze up and down the shires and villages and in every soot-encrusted city in England. Lads who had never attended a real prizefight knew the names of every one of the heroes of the ring. Cheap books were printed telling the stories of the lives of the bare-knuckles bruisers of the prize ring, books with names like *Boxiana: Or, Sketches of Ancient and Modern Pugilism*; *Life & Battles of Tom Sayers*; or, from 1788, *The Complete Art of Boxing According to the Modern Method*, authored by someone calling himself "An Amateur of Eminence." These were the treasured books schoolboys kept hidden from the master, for they had saved their own scarce pennies to buy them. They were the cause of countless bloody noses and equally countless whippings with the headmaster's cane.

In the language of the Fancy, "claret" (as blood was called) was apt to spurt from the "claret jug" (nose) with little provocation. This was, after all, a "blood sport," and that's what the people wanted to see. Points were given for "first blood." The tragic downside was that bare-knuckled pugilism at the hands of powerful men could be a deadly game. When a bout of bare-knuckles fistics was to be fought to the end, there was the possibility of death for one of the boxers. Depending on local laws, the winner was charged with either capital murder or manslaughter, and the backers, seconds and even the spectators were liable to be found guilty of aiding and abetting the crime. When death occurred, the fortunate got away with time in prison; the less fortunate had one more public bout, this time with the gallows.

Following a bitter war with Britain, Americans had little use for all things British—including prizefights. According to one account, prizefights were unknown in America following the Revolutionary War. In 1795, Thomas Cooper, a British expatriate from Manchester, wrote in an article called "Cooper's Information Respecting America":

> *You see nowhere in America the disgusting and melancholy contrast, so common in Europe, of vice, and filth, and rags and wretchedness, in the immediate neighbourhood of the most wanton extravagance, and the most useless and luxurious parade. Nor are the common people so depraved as*

Yankee Sullivan. *Lithograph by George Beach, 1844, Library of Congress, LC-DIG-pga-04356.*

> *in Great-Britain. Quarrels are uncommon, and boxing matches unknown in their streets.*

This peaceful era in America would eventually come to an end with the influx of the "depraved" common people migrating to the new land. The lads who worshiped the "Fancy of the Fives Court" would grow into muscled youths ready to show their prowess. Irish lads, strong as oxen, would beat on one another in the streets of the Irish sections of Boston and New York City. The winners would become renowned—before long, renowned enough to have their positions challenged by pugilists from across the Atlantic.

By 1841, America had its own world champion in Tom Hyer, also the son of a prizefighter. Hyer inspired a new era of pugilism. Another champion of the period was a man called "Yankee" Sullivan, an Irish criminal who had been deported to Australia. Coming to New York around 1840, Sullivan began his career as a political enforcer, working with the local purveyors of broken kneecaps to fix elections. He also began promoting and fighting in prizefights. In 1842, a prizefight between two young Irishmen—Christopher Lily and Thomas McCoy—in which Sullivan was a principal, resulted in the brutal slaying of McCoy. Christopher Lily was arrested but managed to break jail. Yankee Sullivan was arrested as an accomplice; he spent two years in the penitentiary before being pardoned.

By this time, other Australian criminals (called "Sydney Ducks") started to pour into San Francisco, the center of the California gold rush. They accumulated in a part of San Francisco christened "Sydney Town," near the waterfront dives and saloons, and soon set about threatening voters and stuffing ballot boxes to elect their own to public office.

Famous though he was, Sullivan found himself unable to shed his underworld associations. He met his end in the late spring of 1856, when the San Francisco Committee of Vigilance arrested him for his involvement in ballot fraud. After writing out a full confession, which named the others involved, he was found dead in his cell. His wound, a large gash to the artery of his upper arm, was said to be self-inflicted—though many thought this was highly suspect.

It must not be forgotten that even though the pugilists had their admirers, the greater part of society viewed the profession as little different than that of a thug or an assassin. Most of America was of puritanical Protestant stock and viewed Roman Catholics, especially the Irish, as little better than heathens. Since a majority of prizefighters were Irish, most Americans would just as soon see them arrested and put in the penitentiary to mull over their wicked ways.

In 1855, the *Cleveland Plaindealer* printed a short essay on the history of American prizefighters, offering advice to young men with (or without) muscles:

> *"Muscle Men."—It may not be out of place to remind those of our young men who are longing for the emoluments attendant upon a pugilistic victory, that those gentlemen who follow the "manly art" as a profession generally came*

John L. Sullivan. *Photograph by Scott Clifton Carby, unknown date, Library of Congress, LC-DIG-pga-00461.*

*to a bad end. The father of Mr. T. Hyer, who enjoyed the distinguished honor of participating in the first ring fight in the United States, died of too much liquor; Belcher Kay died of too much fight; Wm. Poole died of too much bullet; Pandeen died of too much stab; Yankee Sullivan died of too much Vigilance Committee, and they are continually dropping off, coming to a violent and disgraceful end, unhonored and uncared for. Avoid, therefore, the prize ring, not merely as actors, but as spectators. Black boots—become*

# INTRODUCTION

*an itinerant dealer in tin ware, a free love lecturer, or a woman's rights scribbler—sell pea nuts, study law, or become a local editor, but don't, for the sake of yourselves, or friends, become a pugilist.*

By looking back through old news databases and perusing dusty volumes, I get the feeling that by the early years of the 1880s, a great wave of boxing mania had washed over America. Newspapers began to do blow-by-blow reports on prizefights—because they sold papers. Two-bit paperback biographies of every great pugilist, living or dead, were sold at the corner cigar stand to be purchased by boys of all sizes and walks—from illiterate urchins to spindly armed scholars. By the end of the decade, American cities of any size sported at least one athletic club where members could punch themselves senseless (Queensberry rules, of course). It was also during the 1880s that boxing gloves started to come into fashion in American boxing matches. There was a period when a match could be fought either way, with Queensberry rules signifying gloves and a few other guidelines and London prize ring rules signifying the bare knuckles and dirty tricks of the old prize ring.

It was also during this period that heavyweight prizefighting was dominated by the most famous boxer of that century: John L. Sullivan. Sullivan won the title in 1882 from Paddy Ryan and reigned for the next decade. The handsome, outspoken Sullivan was a sort of man's man. He was the super-American of his time—beefy, good looking, itching for a fight and blind with prejudice and pride. His refusal to fight a black man may indeed have risen from an aversion to mixing races, but it also may have simply been a strong fear of being beaten by a black man, a humiliation he thought he could never outlive.

Sullivan's popularity did much to soften the social attitude toward prizefighters—maybe not with Sunday school teachers but with hard-boiled editors and other sinners with influence. By the end of the century, Sullivan's open and friendly relationship with Theodore Roosevelt had put the blue ribbon of presidential approval on his chest.

In Portland, the 1870s public boxing matches were often the domain of vaudeville's comedic gymnasts, as evidenced by the 1877 appearance of the "Rentz Female Minstrels, Can Can Dancers, and Prize Fight" at the Turner Theater, a ballroom on Fourth and Yamhill Street. Genuine, blood-gushing prizefighting was reserved for cities like New Orleans or New York, where in the wee hours of the night steamboat loads of cigar-smoking men headed for unnamed locations up dark and lonesome rivers.

Many ingenious ways to avert laws against prizefights would come into use. Boxing survived by its unique ability to transform itself from a "disgraceful and barbarous slaughter" into a vaudeville act, a "glove contest," a "friendly bout," a "scientific exhibition" or part of the curriculum at the local athletic association. By the twentieth century, boxing had lost some of its repugnance (although prizefighting, per se, would remain illegal for years). In magazines and newspapers from 1870 through to the end of the century, one can see a lightening up toward the pugilist sports. By 1890, some cities were allowing newly formed "athletic associations" to give exhibitions called "glove contests." As rules based on the Queensberry rules moderated the bloodshed, the name "prizefighter" was no longer synonymous with "murderer." The "glove contest," however, often had every appearance of being a prizefight, and the same lowlife gamblers, bookies and gangsters would gather like carrion birds. This was America, where "the pursuit of happiness" was part of the Declaration of Independence. If droves of people pursued happiness by attending brutal, gladiatorial sports, fueled by alcohol and gambling fever, how could they be denied such pleasure simply because it was seen as low and degrading?

My focus in this book is the time between the first London prize ring prizefights in Portland in the early 1880s and the development of less

An example of an illegal world championship match being held outdoors. John L. Sullivan v. Jake Kilrain, Richburg, Mississippi, 1889. *Library of Congress, LC-USZ62-78648.*

dangerous versions of gloved matches in the 1890s. I am also interested in bringing to light those heroes of the ring who made Portland their home. Some of them, like Dave Campbell and Jack "Nonpareil" Dempsey, were truly heroes, rising above the lowlife image bestowed on most pugilists and helping to make a safer and more acceptable sport for the public to enjoy. These two names should be close to the heart of any lover of Portland history, for in spite of their talent for knocking their opponents out of the ring, they were brave men of humble mind and generous nature. This is not to disparage Amos Smith, the "Mysterious" Billy Smith, whose life was a story of violence and survival matched by few other men in those closing days of the Wild West.

# 1

# The Moonlight Excursion, Being a Narrative Based on Several Reports

Shortly after midnight on October 9, 1883, a young officer of the Portland Police walked his beat with a growing sense of unease. For several nights, he had noticed groups of men talking excitedly together until one of them spotted his uniform. They would then assume positions of nonchalance until he passed, making his face sting red with the insolence of their open secrecy. He couldn't begin to imagine what mischief they were planning, but since many of them were known gamblers, he assumed it had to do with betting large sums of money.

This night was quieter than usual and bitterly cold. Groups of men were no longer hanging around in front of the saloons, and the doors to the rowdy music halls were closed against the chill air. As he walked up Yamhill Street, he chanced to see two shadowy figures disappearing down an alley. He blew his whistle and took chase, but they were absorbed by the darkness.

Several minutes later, he spotted three men hurrying down Salmon Street toward the ferry landings. He went after them, intent to bring them to police court for being out after midnight for no good purpose, but after catching a whiff of what he knew must be very expensive cigar smoke, he abandoned the pursuit. He knew better than to harass gentlemen with well-cut overcoats and dollar cigars.

At about 12:45 a.m., his luck changed. He rounded the corner of Stark and Third and came face to face with a stealthy figure moving briskly along in the shadows.

"Ah, ha!" the officer cried, grabbing the shoulder of what turned out to be an underfed youth of about eighteen years of age.

**MOONLIGHT EXCURSION.**

**Will start promptly from ———**

**on Sunday night, Oct. 14.**

**Tickets $5.**

***Relect.***

Moonlight Excursion. *From* Morning Oregonian, *October 16, 1883.*

"Hey! What are you stopping me for?" the kid said loudly in the voice of one offended.

"Where do you think you are going at this hour of the night?" Officer James demanded.

"I am going on a moonlight excursion," the youth whined, rummaging in his pockets. "Here!" he said, pulling a piece of printed material out of his pocket. It was a ticket of sorts, printed on a jobber press. It read:

> *MOONLIGHT EXCURSION*
> *Will start promptly from__________*
> *on Sunday night, October 9*
> *Tickets $5*

"Moonlight excursion," the policeman read aloud slowly. He glanced up at the cover of clouds. "There ain't no moonlight tonight."

"It don't make no difference," the kid argued. "I got to go. The boat's gonna leave without me."

"It don't say what ferry dock," the officer pressed on.

"It's the one at the end of C," the kid shot back. "Can I go, Mister?"

"Wait! How did you know it was C Street?" the officer demanded.

"I asked Howie at Danzinger's Cigars, where I bought the ticket. Now can I go?"

The policeman smelled a rat, but he could think of no good pretext to detain the lad. He followed as the young man and his shadow moved hurriedly toward the river. At the foot of C Street, an inclined ramp led down to a warehouse and double-decked wharf. The steamboat *Traveler*, alight with lamps and glowing cigars, was being untied from its mooring.

There was a tinkling of the engineer's bell and a short blast of the whistle, and in a burst of white steam the vessel moved into the river. The policeman checked his watch—it was 1:00 a.m., straight up.

The passenger list of the *Traveler* was a few souls shy of one hundred, and according to a wandering reporter, among them was an unusually high percentage of prizefighting experts—or so it seemed by the conversations. Experts or not, many of the "excursionists" had purchased tickets without even a notion of who the pugilists were or where the fight would take place.

As soon as the vessel was away from the dock, an old fellow—known as "Diamond" and described as "a poor, dilapidated specimen of humanity"—pulled a banjo out from under his overcoat and commenced strumming. The geezer had obviously planned to serenade a captive audience, but the audience would have none of it. He was told to "dry up" or he would be thrown overboard. Persuaded by these threats, "Diamond" disappeared into a group of reporters and remained quiet.[1]

The first order of business with the passengers was to discover who the fighters were secreted in cabins below deck. Speculation was running high, with every famous pugilist known to be on the Pacific Coast being named at one point or another. The name Morrissey was mentioned several times by the crowd, as was (by some naïve persons) the name John L. Sullivan. Every well-known bruiser thought to be on the Pacific Coast was pulled out of the hat—until the *Traveler* pulled past the last outskirts of town marked by the steaming smokestacks of the North Pacific Lumber Company and into the narrow channel along Mock's Crest. At this point, the "auctioneer," as the man taking the wagers was called, cried out the names of the pugilists and the odds.

"Our contestants for this battle will be the well-known Billy Morgan, reigning champion of Oregon, thirty-two years of age, standing at five feet, eight inches and 143 pounds, in the pool at ten dollars. His opponent is a newcomer to the prize ring: Tom Manning, thirty years of age, standing at five feet, seven inches, 151 pounds, in the pool at eight dollars. Line up and place your money!"

A visible pall of disappointment fell on the sporting men. Morgan was well known, all right. He had been the bartender at a saloon frequented by the sporting set. He had given "sparring exhibitions" up and down the Northwest and had apparently picked up Manning in Walla Walla. It was claimed that this was Manning's first fight, but for those sober enough to remember, Manning had appeared with Morgan several months earlier at Portland's New Market Theater in what was advertised as "The Manly Art of Self Defense: Sparring and Knocking Out Exhibition."[2]

## NEW TO-DAY

# GLOVE CONTEST

There will be a Ten Round Glove Contest at Liberty Hall on Saturday Evening, the 13th Inst. between

**THOS. WARD**

Champion of Oregon,

AND

**ALBERT JOHNSON**

Middle-weight Champion of Astoria

This contest will begin at 8' o clock.

Larry Sullivan,
Martin Leonard,
Jas. Dyer and,
Jas. McCarron

will also take part

Tickets of Admission - - 50 Cents
Reserved Seats - - - One Dollar

Ward and Johnson Fought the hardest contested prize fight ever fought on the Pacific coast, at Harrignton's Point, theree years ago.

A glove contest. *Facsimile of an advertisement in the* Daily Morning Astorian, *August 9, 1887.*

The show, a lame, pseudo-educational display of fistic techniques, was sandwiched in between Kennedy and Kelly's Original Clog Dances and the Leo Brothers' comic antics. Hearing this, some of the passengers seemed to lose interest in betting, and others demanded to know if this would be a "genuine prizefight." The auctioneer was accustomed to soothing the fears of angry crowds, having sold snake oil for most of his working life. He spoke of how Morgan was the "featherweight champion of Oregon" and how Manning had boxed in the National Guard at Walla Walla, making a big name for himself in that part of the Washington Territory. When the betting was closed, only $230 had been placed.

As the *Traveler* churned past Saint Johns, the full moon broke through the clouds, as advertised, giving a dreamlike quality to the cold night. A group of men gathered in the bow had actually allowed Diamond to drag out his "instrument of torture" and were now singing Stephen Foster ditties to his flailing. The bar and lunch counter opened up for business on the lower decks, but those who remained outside could watch the moonlit waters below and the twinkling milky way rotating almost imperceptibly in the vault of heaven above.

Past the Post Office Bar lights, the *Traveler* moved into the wide waters of the Columbia—flecked with autumn moonlight—and headed in the direction of Astoria. At about 3:00 a.m., those passengers anticipating several hours' sleep were rudely awakened. The steamboat had been traveling close to the shore on the Washington Territory side and was now pulling up to a rickety wharf next to a flickering navigation light. The location, someone said, was Knapp's Landing; there was nothing to be seen in the moonlight but dark groves of trees at the far end of the field and the smoke of a distant chimney.

Some of the men involved in the details went ashore and began setting up a regulation ring, an effort that took multiple measuring attempts and several heated arguments. During this setup period, the moon slid over the horizon, and a chill fog rolled up the river, compelling some passengers to retreat back to the warmth of the steamboat cabin. By 6:00 a.m., the morning light had slowly filled the sky, bringing the sleepy-eyed audience out of the refuge again and onto the shore. The pugilists were up and off together on a walk to shake off the night.

They returned talking and laughing with each other like the best of friends and then separated to disrobe into the fighting costumes beneath their clothes. A Portland buffoon named Henry Griffin—a scrawny little fellow—had been walking up and down challenging to a fight anyone who weighed more than 180 pounds, if he would bring his weight down to Griffin's size before the battle. Having been ignored—without even a chuckle or a groan from the gathering—Griffin slunk off to join a flotsam of salty geezers who seemed to tolerate his presence. The attendants of the fighters busied themselves, bringing out the stools, towels, buckets and other necessary items for the fight to commence.

In a highly democratic move, the entire group was called upon to help appoint the various positions. Jack Dowd—the personable, reformed bunco shark—was chosen, by a large majority, as referee. "Colonel" Joe Taylor, the well-known publican and sportsman, was appointed timekeeper. The two fighters were brought forward and interviewed by "Colonel" Joe about their history. After announcing their age, height and weight, each fighter stepped forward and described his past and his experience in the ring.

Billy Morgan, a well-built man with curling mustaches, said he was born in Ireland thirty-two years earlier. He started fighting, he said, after coming to America. His first match was in 1868 against John Jones of St. Louis. He won the match in seventeen rounds, and he was seventeen years old at the time. He fought Dave Tompkins in Kansas City in 1869. He was beaten after twenty-seven rounds. In 1873, he fought George Sharp in Mission San Jose. The battle was raided by the police in the twenty-seventh round. He whipped Bob Lewis, whom he claimed was the "lightweight champion of London," after four rounds in Livermore. The previous autumn, he had fought with J.K. Mount of Eugene, the fight coming to a draw after thirty-eight rounds. Morgan was known to most of the crowd. He had been in Portland for several years, tending bar at the Palace Saloon and sparring at "Colonel" Joe Taylor's place and some of the other theater saloons of the north end. Morgan wore a sleeveless shirt and slippers without spikes—an oversight that he regretted, having already slipped several times on the wet ground.

Thomas Manning appeared to be a larger man than Morgan and seemed a good deal heavier than his stated statistic of 151 pounds. He was obviously not used to public speaking, but it was ascertained that he had been a private in the First Cavalry at Walla Walla. He said this was to be his first match, a statement that drew some guffaws from the crowd. He was bull necked, muscular and mature, looking ten years older than his stated thirty years. He was stripped to the waist and wore shoes with spikes.

Jack Dowd stepped forward and announced that the crowd should refrain from cheering, jeering or making loud comments during the rounds. The match would be fought according to London prize ring rules—without gloves. The match would continue for as many rounds as it took to bring one

Dave Campbell in pugilistic attire. *Courtesy of Oregon Historical Society, 000956.*

of the contestants down, with thirty seconds between rounds. At 6:35 a.m., in the words of a sleep-deprived reporter, "Morgan 'shied his castor into the ring'[3] and then was joined by Manning in that enclosure."[4] Seconds later, time was called. The two contestants shook hands like old friends, and then, as their grasps loosened, each went into a defensive position.

From the first sound of fist hitting flesh, a hush fell on the crowd. The sound itself seemed to carry with it the weight of transgression—here were adult men smashing each other with their fists, intending to subdue the other by violence. Some of the more naïve among the audience grew uneasy as they considered the fact that, if one were to kill the other, all those in attendance would be held accountable. Be that as it may, they were breaking the law even now by standing in this field of battle.

During the first quarter hour or so, the men were bashing each other enthusiastically, one or the other being knocked to his knees, either from the force of his own blows or those rained down by his opponent, although Morgan slid in the grass more than Manning due to his lack of spikes. This was no exhibition of the fistic sciences; this was a backyard slugfest. Both men were beginning to feel the damage done to them. Morgan had developed an irritating pattern of circling, dashing in for an attack and then sliding to his knees before a return blow could be given. Even with London prize ring rules, it was still a foul to hit a man who was down.

The fight moved briskly, with each round being only about sixty seconds in length. By the twentieth round, Morgan was showing signs of fatigue but jumped back into the ring with apparent vigor when time was called. By the sixtieth round, both men were staggering, but Morgan needed the help of his seconds to move to and from his corner when time was called. In the last quarter of the fight, Manning was in the lead, knocking Morgan about with such veracity that Morgan was often too weak to pull off his attack-and-fall tactic. Soon, his seconds and attendants were begging him to give it up, but on he went, determined to take the full dose of his medicine. By the ninety-ninth round, it was plain that Morgan had had enough. One of his attendants threw in the sponge, and the fight was over. Both contestants managed to walk upright to the middle of the ring, where they shook hands in the same friendly manner as before.

Morgan was reported to have said to Manning at this point, "You're a good man, Tom, and too big for me." The crowd cheered, a hat was passed to provide the loser with some compensation for his struggles and the spectators gave generously. The fight had been a tame one by nineteenth-century standards, with both men receiving a few bruises and Morgan a

**NEW TO-DAY**

**Announcement Extraordinary!**

The Champion's Triumphal Tour
Across the Continent

**THE GREAT**

**JOHN L. SULLIVAN**

**COMBINATION**

**Will Exhibit at OCCIBENTAL HALL**

**On FRIDAY, FEBRUARY 1,**

This great combination embraces the best known and most famous boxers and athletes living, among whom are, first :

JOHN L. SULLIVAN, Champion of the world,

HERBERT A. SLADE, the great Maori Giant,

STEVE TAYLOR, ex- champion heavy-weight of the United States,

PETE McCOY, champion light-weight of America,

MIKE GILLESPIE, Boston's favorite sparrer,

FRANK MORAN, mater of ceremonies,

J. MUNINGER, and other celebrities.

Scenes of the famous Madison Square, New York contest, re-enacted by SULLI_ VAN and Slade

**Special attention will be given to ladies.**

**ADMISSION - - - $1.50**

No extra charge for reserved seats, at the New York Novelty Store.

Al. F. Smith, Manager of Combination.

F.W. Stechtran, Manager Oregon, Washington and British Columbia.

John L. Sullivan in Astoria. *Facsimile of an advertisement in the* Daily Morning Astorian, *February 1884.*

black eye. One of the reporters mentioned that on any given day in the police court, men could be seen in far worse shape than these.

The passengers stepped through the soggy weeds and back to the wharf, where the engineer was tinkling his bell. After a short blast of the whistle, which shot a white geyser of steam into the air, the *Traveler* headed back to Portland. Many of the passengers, though disappointed with the ordinariness of the ordeal, had made the most of it, keeping their complaints to themselves. An *Oregonian* reporter was not so reserved. In his brief mention of the affair, he complained of the misery of going without "a wink of sleep, and with only a cup of coffee and a sandwich, to stand in the wet grass for an hour and a half in the gray dawn of a foggy, chilly autumn morning." He concluded that by the end of the match, everyone was "heartily tired of the affair, and in five minutes after the sponge was thrown up the ground was deserted and the boat on her way home."[5]

This was reported in the *Oregonian* as being Portland's first "genuine prizefight." There had been others before this—quiet barnyard affairs without anyone in attendance literate enough to write about them.

# 2

# The Fistic Fever Sets In

A few weeks after the "moonlight excursion," Billy Morgan, Tom Manning and a handful of Portland amateurs appeared at the Good Templar's Hall to brave what was advertised as a "Knock Out Match." A dismal showing of about one hundred pugilist enthusiasts came to watch. The *Oregonian*'s new self-proclaimed boxing critic described the evening under the headline "Not Knocked Out." By the time the program was half over, he declared that "the affair had grown tiresome by then" and summarized the event by saying sarcastically:

> *It would seem as if the public taste has not been educated up to slugging matches here, and it may be well for the promoters of such affairs to wait awhile before they try to make their fortunes at the prize ring racket.*[6]

Judging from the boxing mania that was already hitting the area, it may have been a better idea for the reporter to hold off judgment on the sport until he had seen a few more matches.

A year or so earlier, a Portland man named F.W. Strechan had sold out his partnership in the D.W. Prentice & Co. Music Store to take over the management of the New Market Theater. Strechan had two aspects to his personality that would make him a success: 1) he believed in giving audiences what they wanted and 2) he was cautiously ambitious, with his ambitions reaching beyond the city of Portland. He started out by presenting to Portland the sort of concerts that would be well received by that portion

A humorous scene of a KOed boxer being carried away. *From H.C. Miner Lithographing Co., 1890, Library of Congress, LC-USZ62-78648.*

of society given to East Coast cultural pretentions: classical concerts, operas and the like. By the time 1884 arrived, Strechan had worked out deals with theaters and promoters in Astoria, San Francisco, Seattle and Victoria, British Columbia, making it possible to book acts of international fame into a Pacific Northwest tour. One of the first acts Strechan booked to tour the circuit he had set up was world-renowned pugilist John L. Sullivan—a name that brought admiration to the hearts of all red-blooded, cigar-chomping whiskey guzzlers throughout the land.

Just a few short weeks after the article denouncing boxing in Portland appeared in the *Oregonian*, the great John L. Sullivan came to town. Sullivan, quite possibly the most popular man alive at the time, was on a four-month tour, under the management of Al F. Smith, along with an entourage of famous and semi-famous prizefighters. It was not advertised as a "prizefight," though Sullivan brought with him an entire sideshow of "glove scientists" for "demonstration purposes." One can be sure the chief of police would watch over the event with a cautious eye, and if it started to look too much like a prizefight (i.e., if it got too bloody), he would shut it down.

At the time of this tour, John L. Sullivan was at the height of his fame and was mentioned in the national press nearly every day. Thanks to the fairly recent train service connecting the continental states, Sullivan and his "combination" was able to travel rapidly around the country—from Boston across the northern states through Denver and Helena to San Francisco. From there, he moved to Astoria, then Portland, then Seattle and Victoria, back to Portland, then back to San Francisco and across the Southwest and South. The telegraph wires hummed with the latest gossip relating to Sullivan's many brushes with the law and other difficulties arising from his love of alcohol and loss of reason when in a drunken rage. If Sullivan conducted himself as a gentleman during a visit, it was not beyond the scruples of many an ambitious newspaperman to invent a lively story. According to the reports, he did many cowardly things—beating up smaller men without cause, refusing to fight local talent, wrecking barrooms and so on. As many admirers as Sullivan had, he also had many detractors who would relish seeing the famous Bostonian brought low. It was the policy of many newspapers at the time to give the public what they wanted, whether the story was an actual event or an event taking place in the imagination of an ambitious hack.

At the beginning, and throughout this tour, Sullivan made it clear that he would fight anyone for a $1,000 prize if his opponent could remain upright in the ring for four rounds—Queensberry rules. After endless requests by young toughs who imagined themselves champions, Sullivan stated, "I have given up fighting under London prize ring rules, and I have done meeting chumps."[7]

Even though Sullivan had won his world championship fight against Paddy Ryan under London prize ring rules it had become acceptable (due to pressure from authorities) for prizefights to be conducted under Queensberry rules, although many matches were still being challenged under the former bare-knuckles arrangements. Sullivan was probably tired of having matches interrupted by the police, for by this time Queensberry rules indicated a "glove contest," and bare knuckles indicated a bloody fight to the end, with serious injury or death a strong possibility. Even so, there were still police chiefs who could care less about the appellation "glove contest" and monitored each performance for indications that some sort of serious pugilistic warfare was taking place.

Most of the boxing antics that Portlanders had seen up to the time of Sullivan's "glove contest" were performed by local ruffians and pugilists who claimed to be champion of some nearby state or territory. Billy Morgan was good, and he was in Oregon; therefore, he was the "champion of Oregon" until someone knocked his block off. The contenders were many, but the publicity was scarce. Many a soon-forgotten "championship" bout was fought in a barnyard or down the river from Portland on a barge. There was little notice taken of differences in weight and height between contestants in the ring in those days, with welterweights sometimes laying heavyweights out flat (if not the other way around).

On February 1, 1884, Sullivan's "combination" arrived in Astoria from San Francisco aboard the steamer SS *Oregon*. So far on the tour, Sullivan had met with six men who had accepted the $1,000 challenge,[8] all of them having been knocked silly after a short bout in the ring. Astoria, not to be bested for having the toughest men alive, offered a gigantic mangler named Sylvester Growriff as a contestant for the $1,000 challenge. Even though Growriff lasted only twenty seconds into the match, the Astoria crowd was highly appreciative of the evening's presentations.[9]

Two days later, the Sullivan troupe arrived in Portland aboard the steamboat *Fleetwood* from Astoria. The hero was met by a cheering crowd and a band of policeman. The police kept the crowd at bay while leading the Sullivan troupe to the Esmond Hotel. The troupe's visit to the New Market Theater was received by an enthusiastic crowd. Even though earlier reports from the tour had described the event as disappointing and nothing more than a vaudeville show, the mighty, muscular John L. Sullivan moved about the ring with the grace of an African gazelle, with ballet-like footwork and the "liver pads" on his mighty fists pummeling his opponent with the speed of a jackhammer. An *Oregonian* reporter described the event in these words:

The great pugilist Francis Archibald Kelhead Douglas, tenth Marquis of Queensberry. *Photograph by George G. Bain, 1896, Library of Congress LC-USZ62-83086.*

> *It was a good natured, well-behaved audience, quick to catch a good point, and as quick to applaud it. Everyone seemed to recognize that he came to see only an exhibition, not a prize-fight, and no one was disappointed because blood was not drawn nor features bruised.*[10]

After traveling up to Seattle and Victoria, Al Smith and F.W. Strechan brought the Sullivan troupe back to Portland on February 15 to catch the many sports lovers who were unable to buy tickets to the previously sold-out house. The event was nevertheless anticlimactic, receiving only brief mention in the newspapers.

By the time the John L. Sullivan troupe showed up in Portland, it was plain that few of the local boys had the necessary "sand" to stand up to the professionals in the ring—with one important exception: Dave Campbell, a twenty-one-year-old volunteer fireman from Portland. Campbell is described as the "perfect Adonis" who had come to the attention of the local boxing promoters because of his incredible strength and natural ability in the ring. Rumors existed that Campbell had already seen some prizefighting prior to what was described as "Campbell's first fight."[11] There were rumors abounding about Campbell having fought two "steamboat excursion" prizefights "down the Columbia" as the protégé of Joe Taylor, a large barkeep with the appropriate name of J.E. "Jumbo" Reilly. Joe Taylor, it may be recalled, was the owner of a saloon theater in the north end called Joe Taylor's Place, where pugilistic exhibitions were permitted. The rumor mill had it that Campbell had defeated "Jumbo" Reilly in the fourteenth round in the first fight, with no details to be discovered of the second bout except that Campbell was victorious.

In June, Dave Campbell was booked into the Mechanic's Pavilion in Portland to fight Pete Lawler, a prizefighter from New York who had become the acknowledged "Pacific Coast Champion," mostly fighting in California. The fight was a bigger hit by far than the recent John L. Sullivan tour. The Mechanic's Pavilion had room for one thousand spectators, compared to the three hundred maximum of the New Market Theater—the popularity of the sport having gone up considerably since the appearance of John L. At the beginning of the match, the referee handed the gloves to Portland police chief Samuel B. Parrish for his examination. He then laid the gloves at each corner and let the "Queensberry rules glove contest" begin.

The first round was a slow start, with a cautious, pale Campbell blocking Lawler's thrusts in a manner that seemed almost clumsy. Some of the crowd said they even felt sorry for the twenty-one-year-old Portland firefighter who seemed like a good-looking kid next to the older, much heavier, tanned and muscular Lawler. Then Campbell knocked Lawler into the ropes with a heavy blow to his chin. The second-round bell had just been rung when it became apparent that Campbell had marked Lawler's weak spot and seemed intent on damaging his chin once more. It seemed like the round had been going for mere seconds when Campbell landed a lightning punch on Lawler's chin with his right and another thunderous blow with his left glove to Lawler's ear. The big prizefighter fell on his face like a dead man. The referee declared the match a knockout, and the crowd went wild. Lawler's trainer, Jack O'Neil, and his second, pugilist Tom Manning, carried

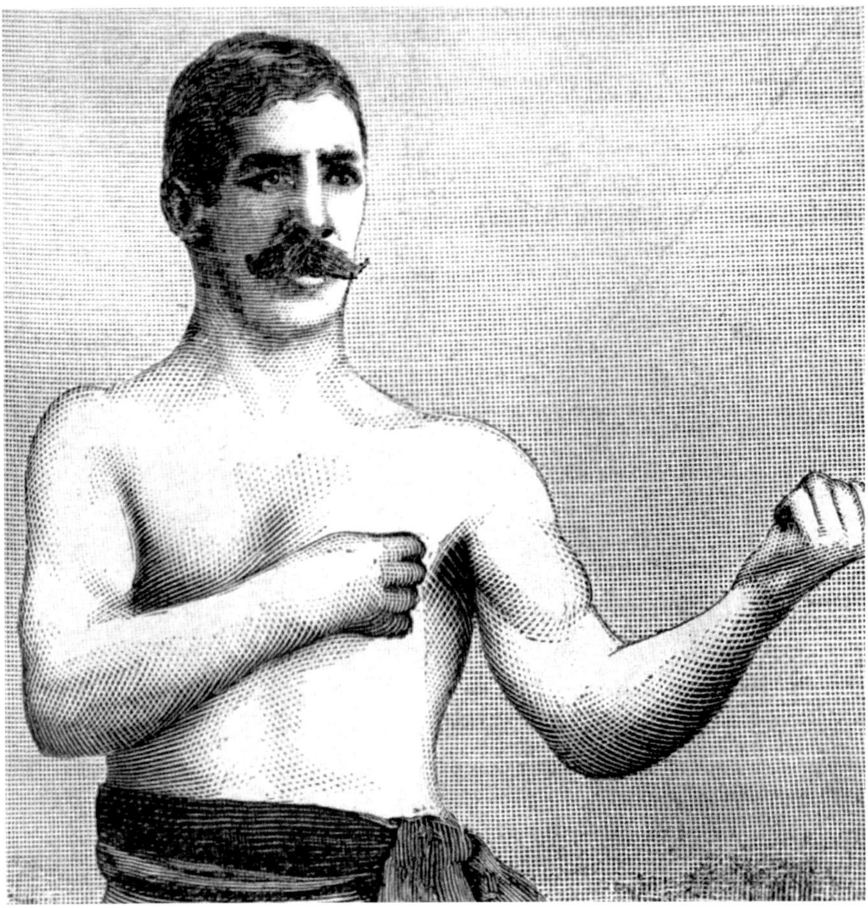

Billy Manning. *From Richard K. Fox,* Life and Battles of Jack Dempsey, *1889.*

the fallen gladiator to his dressing room, followed by a squad of policeman. Fortunately for Campbell, his opponent came back to consciousness within a few minutes, describing his experience to reporters as "first dizziness, and then a complete blackout."

The police chief was there to call a halt to the event should it start to draw an overabundance of blood or cause visible injury, but he may have been so caught up in the spirit of the moment that he failed to notice when the line was crossed in the blink of an eye. He is hardly to be blamed, however, since the contest was over almost as fast as it began, with the added bonus of not having any serious injuries. Had Lawler been injured or, God forbid, killed, then Chief Parrish would have been compelled to arrest the new hero in the midst of his celebrations. This would not have gone over well with voters or the members of civil society to whom the chief had to answer. That Campbell was now Portland's darling, admired more than almost any other local figure of the day, can be seen in the following quote from an ecstatic reporter in the next morning's paper: "It matters not now whether the new hotel is ever built or not, whether a bridge ever crosses the Willamette, or the Columbia bar is improved. Portland can rest on last night's glory."[12]

# 3

# A Dogfight with Frenchmen

There was a period of pugilistic peace following Campbell's victory over Lawler. It may be that there were some more "excursions" downriver, but if there were, they were kept quiet from the papers and the general public. Dave Campbell seemed to be rolling along unconcerned about his career possibilities in the world of man-punchers. The only fight that came to the public's attention that winter was a fight between Campbell's dog and the dogs of two "Frenchmen" that turned into into a mêlée among the humans. The whole affair cost Campbell a little dignity and ten dollars' forfeited bail for a charge of disorderly conduct.

Summertime breathed new life into the Portland scene. Word was out that Dave Campbell had signed papers to fight young J.E. "Jumbo" Reilly. The coals were further bellowed to life by the arrival of an enormous, bearded grizzly bear of a kilt-wearing Scotsman by the name of Duncan McDonald. The Caledonian was a once famous, now retired wrestler and prizefighter who had transformed himself into a professor of martial arts. He had broken his arm in the twenty-fourth round of a prizefight in Butte, Montana, and had ended up staying. He had come to Portland to train Dave Campbell for his upcoming match. Duncan moved his new student down to the White House at the end of Macadam Road. From there, he could oversee the physical training of his student without the interruptions of life in town and with the almost sadistic rigor of a true Scotsman.

By late August, other members of the national fisticuffs society had started to show up in town. Reilly had engaged a little-known pugilist from

Scranton, Pennsylvania, named Larry Sullivan to be his trainer. All that was known about the young man was that he claimed John L. Sullivan was his uncle and that he, Larry Sullivan, could whip any man on the Pacific Coast. It wasn't long before Reilly gave his arrogant tutor the boot. The disgruntled Sullivan sulked around town until he found lucrative employment as a "runner" for a sailor's boardinghouse in Astoria run by the infamous Jim Turk. It was the job of a runner to find men who could be cheated, tricked or convinced by other means to drop what they were doing to join the ranks of mariners.[13] Reilly then replaced Larry Sullivan with the tried and true talents of Portland's own favorite publican, trainer and promoter of pugilists: old Joe Taylor.

Between the hours of 2:00 and 3:00 a.m. on the morning of September 12, 1885, crowds of men could be seen moving stealthily through the darkness of downtown Portland toward the ferry docks. There, the steamboats *Salem* and *Lucea Mason* lay waiting, their lanterns burning low, engines throbbing quietly. Promptly at 3:00 a.m., the vessels let loose quick bursts from their steam whistles, their great paddle wheels churning the dark river into a froth. At the same time at the mouth of the Columbia River, in the dimly lighted streets of Astoria, men were winding their way to the dock where the steamboat *Tom Morris* was being readied for an excursion. It was a fine night in September, the finest month of the year. The heat of August had been blown off by the pleasant tang of marine air, and the rains of October were yet to come. The sleep-deprived crowds of men set out on the waters, above them billows of pure white steam shooting into the dark and all around them clouds of fragrant cigar smoke perfuming the air like a sultan's garden. The navigational post lanterns along the shore, the stars above and the lights of the steamboats moved together to the rhythmic music of the engines below, driving the steamboats across the surface of the dark waters.

At dawn, the Portland steamboats arrived at a landing near a sandy shore in Clark County, on the Washington Territory side of the Columbia River. Waiting for them there, in the semidarkness, was a small steamboat and a group of men. It turned out the men were a posse put together by Clark County sheriff L.B. Clough at the direction of the Clark County commissioners for the purpose of thwarting prizefights on the Washington Territory shore.[14] After some heated discussion, the *Salem* and *Lucea Mason* moved off with angry blasts of the whistles, as if to return to Portland, though they soon changed course back downstream. Joe Taylor sent a boy around telling the excursionists that there was a spot downriver where they could fight 'til kingdom come.

**NEW TO-DAY**

**THE "CLARA PARKER"**

Will Leave the Dock of Sunday Evening, November 1st, 1885 for the

**CAMPBELL -- DEMPSEY,**

AND

**Ward--Sullivan, Prize Fights.**

**Tickets Four Dollars,**

Including Round Trip and Admission to the Ring to Witness Both FIghts. For Sale at the New York Novelty Store and Sunnyside Saloon. TIme ofleaving will be stated Sunday Morning.

Campbell-Dempsey. *Facsimile of an advertisement in the* Daily Morning Astorian, *October 29, 1885.*

The spot turned out to be the Ward ranch, across the Columbia from a point below Saint Helens that was hidden from the main river channel by several uninhabited islands.[15] Here the organizers disembarked and made a path through the thick grasses to a level spot, where they mowed and raked a space large enough for the twenty-four- by twenty-four-foot-square "ring" of the London prize ring regulations. Indeed, the prize ring rules were the reason for this excursion. Had the boxers accepted a Queensberry rules match, it could have been held at a venue in the city—although the purse would have had to have been kept a secret. It seemed that at that time, the authorities in Portland deemed a match could be held using gloves as long as there was no purse connected with the event.

Out here under the whitening sky, filled with the songs of robins and the chatter of sparrows, they could pummel each other with bare fists until one of them could no longer stand under his own power. They could gamble, and they could curse without a policeman's hand landing on their shoulders (and a ten-dollar fine). They could smoke great vaporous clouds of cigar smoke and spit tobacco juice on the grass; they could "hiss" and "boo" or cry out encouragement and advice. They could knock out their hangovers with some stiff belts from a pocket flask. They could walk into the tall grass at the edge of the crowd to relieve themselves. Besides all these joys of late nineteenth-century manhood, there lingered the notion that a prizefight was not really a prizefight that counted unless it was held under London prize ring rules—this despite all the efforts that John L. Sullivan (not to mention all the other admirers of the Marquis of Queensberry's "science") had put forward to change this practice.

About the time the ring was made ready, the *Tom Morris* could be seen chugging upriver, laboring against the current. Soon, the Astoria steamboat was tying up to the *Lucea Mason*, and the men were scrambling over the decks to the gangway. The fight, it was announced, would begin promptly at 9:00 a.m. Dozens of men began checking their watches as Duncan McDonald (Campbell's trainer and second) and old Joe Taylor (Reilly's trainer and second) stepped up to the ring to make last-minute preparations. The purse was a substantial (but not outrageous) $500 apiece, with each contestant putting up his own $100 on top, winner take all. The pool reached $1,550 with Campbell as the favorite, although Joe Taylor and close associates tended to favor Reilly. Outside betting was estimated to be at least $1,000. In the tradition of prize ring rules, the crowd was asked to name a referee. The popular vote went to George Stevens, a well-liked sportsman from Astoria. The last preparation before the match was to take the handkerchiefs (colors) from each contestant to tie on to their prospective corner posts. The winner of the match took the colors as a prize and collected them, sometimes wearing them as a belt.

From pale dawn to the start of the match, time seemed to slow to a dreamlike pace. Slow were the mists that moved away like curtains from the winter blue sky. Slow were the men who walked as if in a ceremony, a dirge, black coats, hats and umbrellas against the same pale morning.

Then, suddenly, "Time!" was called, and the two men were beating on each other in a dreadful manner. After what seemed mere seconds, "Time!" was called again—and again, after a short rest, and the men were back smashing at each other with their fearsome fists. By prize ring rules, the rounds were to last one minute, with resting periods of thirty seconds. By these rules, time flew into high gear, round upon round; Campbell seemed the aggressor, battering Reilly and remaining mostly untouched. Reilly, on the other hand, was a skillful fighter and well versed in defending himself.

Dave Campbell. *From Richard K. Fox,* Life and Battles of Jack Dempsey, *1889.*

At the beginning of the fourteenth round, Reilly came in groggy but still wily enough to try backing Campbell into a corner of the square ring. Campbell, in a controlled rage, placed a crushing blow to Reilly's left cheek, followed by another hammering blow to his chin. This laid Reilly out flat, senseless and unable to rise within the proscribed eight seconds. The bout had happened so fast that it was reported in the *Daily Astorian*[16] as having lasted sixteen minutes when in fact, by prize ring rules, it would have taken twenty-one minutes.

Slowly, the steamboats departed on their routes as the pale day turned crimson. Some of the men were able to snooze aboard a steamboat; other, more squeamish fellows paced the decks or nervously played cards with the card sharks. I am of the opinion, though, that most of the men (unless they stopped in at a dive, like old Joe Taylor's) made it home by suppertime.

# 4

# The "Nonpareil"

The society ladies shuddered at the attention Portland was getting. There had been rumors of fights downriver, but the last one had been infamous, reported in newspapers all over the country. One notorious prizefight was bad enough, but there were so-called glove contests in the Pavilion, the New Market Theater and several large north end saloons and oyster bars—where it was rumored there were no gloves at all. In school, the words "prizefight and Campbell" were on the lips of little boys and big ones. Even in Sunday school, there were questions about the propriety of settling scores with fists and discussions wherein Dave Campbell was compared to Sampson or Goliath.

All this was almost too much for some of the "pious" old settlers who had established themselves comfortably in Portland Heights and on Nob Hill and whose families owned much of the commerce of the city. A mere ten years before this, the *New York Times* had compared Portland, Oregon, to a puritanical New England village. The deeper ship channel, the railroads and other economic factors had turned Portland into a city with inhabitants from as far away as the celestial kingdom of Cathay and with sailors arriving from every part of Queen Victoria's realm. With them they brought their desires and devices—including a remarkable array of vice: prostitution, gambling dens and every other dark pleasure invented by that time. It is a well-known fact that forbidden pleasures are democratic in their appeal to certain people, regardless of social status. What the matrons at the society tea might not have understood was that a good part of the increase in income

The National Police Gazette Building, New York. *From Richard K. Fox,* Life and Battles of Jack Dempsey, *1889.*

that paid for family comfort came from businesses that were fishy, under the table or with persons whose presence would have been scandalous in any of their homes. The husband, in fact, may have spent his evening gambling at one of the clubs after attending the vestry meeting at Trinity Church. Some of the Nob Hill gents, the ones headed for perdition, could even be seen entering one of the "French" bagnios[17] in the north end, and some ended up gazing into space from a pipe dreamer's pallet in one of the hidden rooms of Chinatown. These were men who would not only attend an illegal prizefight, but also some of them would back one of the fighters with real money and even handle his expenses.

## ANOTHER IRISHMAN

After the last fight, the telegraph wires had been humming back and forth between Portland and San Francisco and New York and Portland. Any number of promoters and would-be backers wanted a part of such beautiful raw talent as Dave Campbell. A matchmaker was said to be in California and to have set up Campbell's next match with the brightest star on both coasts: a twenty-two-year-old lad born in Kildare, Ireland, lately from Brooklyn, who went by the name of Jack Dempsey.[18]

Kildare was an ideal spot for a prizefighter to be born. The Curragh of Kildare was a large, open prairie—often a battleground—and it contained a hollow, a natural amphitheater used regularly for prizefighting. It was named Donnely's Hollow after a famous early champion Irish pugilist.

When Jack was in his second year of grammar school, he immigrated to America with his father, mother and a sister. They settled in the Williamsburg section of Brooklyn, where his father was employed in a cooperage shop and young Jack resumed his schooling. After only two years in his new country, Jack's father died of tuberculosis, leaving his son to fend for himself. When the lad was only about ten years old, he took up his father's work, hammering together casks and barrels at his father's old workplace.[19] This he would do for the remainder of his childhood, while other children, from better circumstances, attended school and played games with their chums. In his late teens, Dempsey became a skilled wrestler with a reputation around Williamsburg as an up-and-coming champ.

## RARE CONTEST

The story of how Jack Dempsey became a boxer is an interesting one. It was in 1883, when Dempsey was twenty years old, that, by a twist of fate, he became an overnight champion and started on the road to becoming the world-renowned "Nonpareil."

A young tough named Ed McDonald began presenting himself as the "Champion of New York," giving boxing exhibitions around Brooklyn. In these exhibitions, McDonald would come up against some opponent who was a plant, a "fall guy" with whom he would arrange a simulated knockout. It so happened that one day, as McDonald was readying himself for an "exhibition" at Williamsburg, the fall guy failed to show up. McDonald was in need of a substitute, so someone told him that Jack Dempsey had a reputation as a "collar-and-elbow wrestler."[20] That was good enough for McDonald, who was sure that his "science" as a pugilist would see him lay Dempsey out flat in no time.

The sportswriter for *Pearson's Magazine*, Richard Barry, gives a wonderful description of the arrival of Jack Dempsey, showing how his slight appearance and friendly attitude tended to make his opponents overly confident that he was an easy target:

> *This was but an hour before the opening of the show which was to be held on the second floor of a hotel in a room used sometimes for dancing and sometimes for lodge meetings. About the time the crowd had assembled in loafed Jack Dempsey, a stripling with a handsome face and a most deferential and winning manner.*
>
> *He looked like the last man in the world to seek a fight or provoke a quarrel. His figure was slender and elegant. Were it not for the working clothes he wore he might have been called a "gentleman." He had then—and always—that curious restraint mingled with a jovial alertness which distinguishes the Irishman of good blood. He was the son of a peasant, but only his tough hands and his speech, which he wisely seldom used, indicated a lack of culture. No one talking with him could imagine the genius of battle which slumbered within any more than to look at his body could have guessed the marvelous concentrated power of those essentially pugilistic muscles.*[21]

McDonald then informed Dempsey that he intended to knock him out in the fifth or sixth round, he would not hurt him and he would let him know before it happened. There would be five dollars in it for him. When Dempsey protested, McDonald told him that it was not a disgrace to be knocked out by Ed McDonald. Dempsey was then given a pair of boxing trunks and told not to worry about it.

Dempsey was 130 pounds to McDonald's 160, and he was inexperienced in the ring, but regardless, the fighters seemed evenly matched. For five rounds, the sparring went on, with the spectators cheering for the underdog (Dempsey), as would be expected. McDonald had been unable to land a serious blow on the lad, whose supple movements kept him one step ahead of his opponent's fists. By this time, McDonald was enraged. He had promised to let Dempsey know when he was going to knock him out, but now he decided to go full force on his upstart opponent.

In the sixth round, the spectators could tell the tide had shifted. McDonald came at Dempsey with two powerful blows that would have knocked a man of his size out of the ring. Dempsey dodged them both with expert skill, causing his opponent to nearly lose his balance. McDonald then growled at him that it was time for him to take the fall. Once again, Dempsey protested that he did not care to be knocked out.

The match continued for many more rounds, with Dempsey dodging McDonald's powerful blows. Dempsey was able to punish his opponent with his steady hammering, much like a cooper putting a ring of iron on a barrel. By the twentieth round, McDonald was in serious trouble, looking for a way to escape. But he couldn't throw in the towel—these were the days of fighting to the bitter end, and it was an end he wanted to avoid. He worked his way around the ring until he was near an exit, and there he leapt over the ropes to make an escape, but Dempsey's seconds grabbed him and tossed him back into the ring. The spectators were at a high pitch of excitement by this time, according to Barry. "[E]veryone realized that this was indeed a great fight, one of those rare contests that a man sees but a few times in his entire life."[22]

It was then that McDonald began fighting for all he was worth. The rounds continued, and the blood (McDonald's) began to flow beneath the hammering fists of the Irishman. Once again, according to Barry, the twenty-fifth and the twenty-sixth rounds were "the greatest exhibition of desperate fisticuffs ever seen," wherein the two men "slammed and slugged like demons." Finally, in the twenty-seventh round,[23] McDonald was knocked out cold, counted out and Jack Dempsey became a champion.

## BECOMING THE "NONPAREIL"

This was the beginning of a long stretch of victories for Dempsey over the next two years. The previous February, in the offices of the *National Police Gazette*, he had signed articles to fight Billy Dacey, the lightweight champion of New York, and a few weeks later, George Fulljames, the lightweight championship of Canada. The match was for $2,000 and the *National Police Gazette* lightweight championship[24]—the title that Dempsey held at the time of his arrival in Portland. This match was the first championship match to be decided under the Marquis of Queensberry rules at a time when both

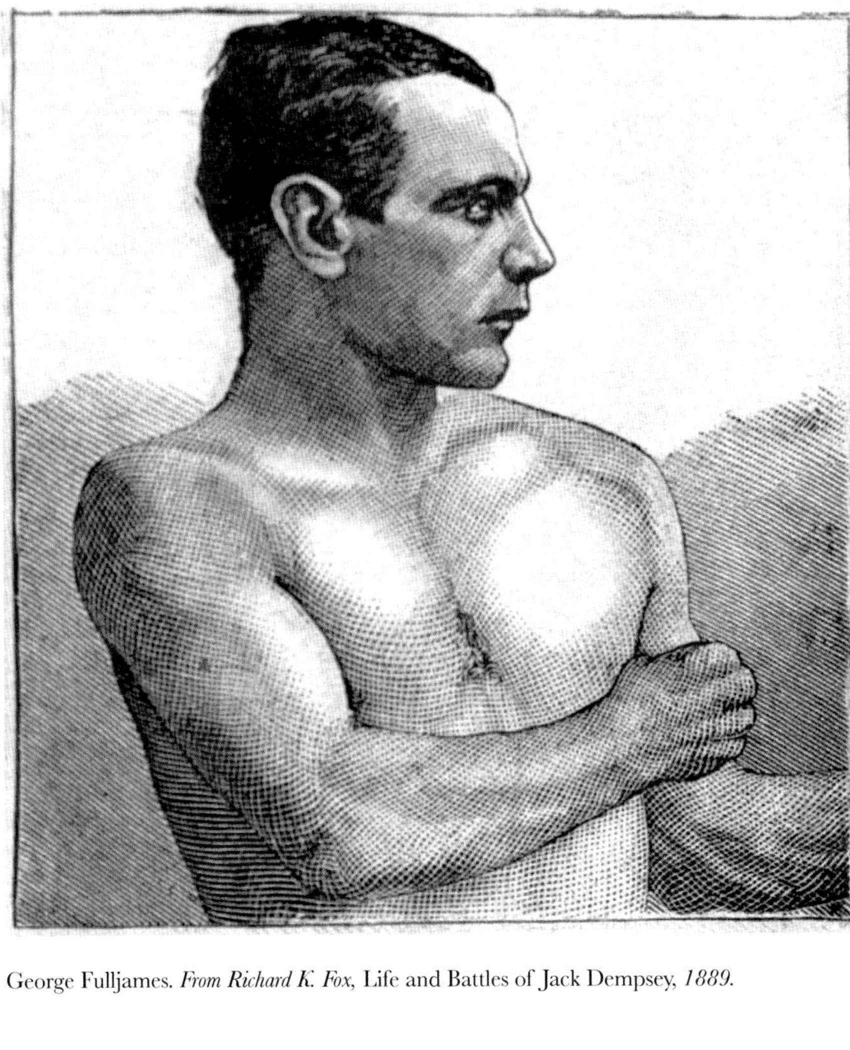

George Fulljames. *From Richard K. Fox,* Life and Battles of Jack Dempsey, *1889.*

rule sets were in use. Dempsey's record was an astounding list of matches that left him unbeaten (for all practical purposes). He had acquired the nickname "Nonpareil" to indicate that he was "beyond parallel"—a tough honor to uphold in a sport where parallels were drawn and redrawn every day. Richard K. Fox, the editor of the *National Police Gazette*, had this to say about Dempsey's style:

> *His style and method of boxing has a neatness about it which is completely new and unknown. He stops blows aimed at him by his adversaries with so much skill, and hits his antagonist with such terrific force and comparative ease, that he astonishes and terrifies his opponents beyond measure.*[25]

Early in the spring of 1885, Dempsey announced that he would make a tour of the states by rail, from "Maine to Oregon," meeting any and all comers at his weight. He traveled via rail, accompanied by his manager, Jake Stern. In March, they arrived in New Orleans, where Dempsey fought the local champion, Charley Bixamos, for $1,000. The blood-covered Bixamos went down on his face in the fifth round.

In San Francisco, Dempsey set about challenging champions and sluggers alike, fighting at the Olympic Club, the Pavilion or Harry Maynard's club. California was well under the sway of prizefight fever, with prominent athletic clubs and sporting dens in Los Angeles, San Francisco and Sacramento and over the mountains in Carson City. So far, Dempsey had retained the appellation "Nonpareil," untarnished by defeat.

At the San Francisco Pavilion, he fought Tom Cleary, a New York boy who had become a Pacific Coast champion. Dempsey demolished the dispirited Cleary in the fifth round.

At the old Wigwam Theater (on the corner of Geary and Stockton, torn down in 1886), Dempsey fought the noted pugilist Jim Carr, knocking him under the ropes after nine gruesome rounds.

That July took him to Carson City, where he met with the Nevada champion, Jim Rodda, under Queensberry rules. After a torturous five minutes and thirty-five seconds, Rodda was knocked cold.

Next, Dempsey found himself challenged by Jack Keenan, a short, bulldog of a man who had claimed the world featherweight championship. The fight was almost impromptu and was fought in Golden Gate Park, London prize ring rules. Keenan was unfortunate in his looks at the best of times—in fact, he was an ugly little fellow—but after coming back round after round for the punishment of Dempsey's fists, he was a sight of horror. Keenan was mangled, groggy and spitting blood when Dempsey became reluctant to hit him any longer.

"I'll be damned if I will quit!" Keenan sputtered through a mouthful of blood.

Dempsey looked helplessly at the crowd. "Can't you make him stop? No? Well if I've got to lick him, I'll lick him damn quick!"[26] He then brought a quick left hook on Keenan's jaw, sending him sprawling.

Later that afternoon at Farley's Saloon, the two fighters met again, shaking hands over a drink. "Damn you, Jack," Keenan spoke through his bruised mouth. "We are friends now, and I like you, but it wasn't right of you to spoil my good looks."

After allowing his hand to heal—he broke it in the match with Keenan—Dempsey was pitted against the famous Englishman, pugilist, fighting instructor and manager Billy Manning. Manning was a great deal older than Dempsey and had won his first prizefight when Dempsey was still in swaddling clothes. Manning had set up shop in San Francisco, where his talents were put to use training fighters in the clubs and dens of pugilism. His talents as a manager were well known as well; Manning managed John L. Sullivan. He had also been Sullivan's sparring opponent in one of Sullivan's moneymaking "glove contest" tours. The match was fought at the San Francisco Turn Halle on August 29, 1885. The hall was well beyond its capacity, stifling hot and misty with a fog of cigar smoke. Dempsey began round four with a crushing left-hand blow directly on Manning's nose, causing it to become a geyser of "claret." The audience was delighted, but Police Chief Benedict stepped onto the stage and demanded the bout be stopped. At this, the crowd went berserk, stamping, shouting and hissing. The referee announced that the fight would have to continue the next day, but the crowd would have none of it. Finally, Chief Benedict gave in, provided the men were given larger gloves.

At the end of round seven, Manning was knocked into a heap but quickly recovered, limping to his chair, bruised and covered with blood. Before the bell could ring again, Chief Benedict returned with reinforcements and demanded the match come to a close. The referee, Charles Schroder, gave the match to Dempsey.

## DEMPSEY COMES TO PORTLAND

Meanwhile, word began to circulate in the City of Roses to the north that the new lightweight champ, Jack "Nonpareil" Dempsey, was coming to fight Dave Campbell. Portland sportsmen had no fear that their champ would be beaten by a lightweight. Campbell was described by many as a giant of a man—a man who, if seen without his shirt, with his muscles gleaming in the sunlight, could take the breath away from spectators of both sexes. If Dempsey came to fight Campbell, Portland's money was on Campbell. The rules of weight were oftentimes stretched in all directions. In San Francisco, Jack Dempsey had weighed 144 pounds, a fact confirmed by the testimony of James J. Corbett, the man who took the heavyweight championship of the world away from John L. Sullivan. When Corbett was a greenhorn lad, he had the opportunity to box a training bout with Dempsey. Dempsey was somewhat contemptuous of the lad, until he made him start to sweat. By the end of the bout, Dempsey was glowing with admiration. Corbett wrote in his autobiography that following the bout, Dempsey had slapped him on the back and said, "Boy, if I was as big as you, I would lick any man in the world!"

Dempsey's first victory versus Ed McDonald. *From Richard K. Fox,* Life and Battles of Jack Dempsey, *1889.*

News of the upcoming fight brought excitement and consternation to Portland. It was noticed by the police (and other persons given to eyeing outlanders with suspicion) that there were new faces lurking about town—faces that belonged to tough-looking characters, gamblers, pickpockets and that sort. An unnamed editorialist for the *Oregonian* voiced the concerns felt by many Portlanders when he wrote a proposal under the heading "SUPPRESS THE PRIZE FIGHT" that called for "hard cheese" to be handed to all involved in prizefighting. One could even go as far as to call the editorialist a "spoil sport." Here are excerpts:

> *For several days there has been high excitement in Portland about a prize fight which, it is said, will take place to-day. The city is full of a class of beings, the hardest that still keep the form of humanity, and more deeply degraded than any creatures known in other than human form, attracted from hundreds of miles, to witness the exhibit...*
>
> *There ought to be a stringent statute making it a felony to arrange a prize fight in the state, to enter into negotiations for arrangement of a prize fight, or to engage in such prize fight in any manner, either as principal, second, assistant, stake-holder, trainer or referee. The statutes should also forbid persons to leave the state to carry on such prize fight or to assist in it in any capacity, and it should empower and direct the officers to make arrests when persons are about to depart on such errands.*
>
> *These regulations, made sufficiently comprehensive and explicit, if they did not stop this disgraceful brutality, at least would compel it to keep under cover. It is now open and shameless. Its publicity is debasing to the last degree. Inasmuch as the legislature will assemble in a few days, it is hoped that a legal remedy may be provided that will check the growing frequency of these brutal occurrences. Every consideration of order, decency and morals requires it.*[27]

Like many other things, prizefighting was something that would go in and out of focus with the anti-vice reformers. As the editorial said, "Keep it under cover." If some vice or another became too visible, the lovers of that vice would soon find themselves under attack. This was, after all, 1885—high Victorian times—and there were few places on earth where Victorianism was more in vogue than in the hinterland city of Portland, Oregon. By the end of the decade, the north part of Portland, where many of the theater saloons, bagnios and gambling dens were located, would be christened "Whitechapel" by newspapermen, a decidedly Victorian touch to the city's reputation.

One thing that would help erode the thug image of local pugilism would be the fact that Dave Campbell was one of the straightest arrows ever made in the likeness of his creator. He was not only handsome, but his appearance was also one of wholesomeness and heroism. He didn't carouse, or at least not to any noticeable level; the man didn't even smoke cigars (he was a fireman, after all).

## DAVID CAMPBELL, THE FEARLESS GIANT

Dave Campbell was born in Pittsburg, Pennsylvania, and was fourteen when he came with his father to Portland. Shortly after his arrival, he went to work as an "expressman" (messenger) and lived on his own wages at the Burton House, a hotel on the corner of Third and F Streets. Here, meals were twenty-five cents, and lodging was twenty-five cents, so whatever he made over a half dollar was his to spend as he liked. Dave Campbell was one of those strong, good-looking, forthright types, instantly liked by most people. As a lad, he carried enough of a punch to keep himself on the good side of the hucksters and vultures that prey on the young and inexperienced. He was given a wide berth by wicked men who had no desire to feel his jackhammer fists. During this period, he followed his original dream—the dream of many a tiny tot—to be a fireman. He hung around the firehouse, making himself useful, until finally he was made a real volunteer fireman.

In the rough world of the nineteenth-century working stiff, whenever there was someone who looked like Goliath the Philistine walking down the street, there was always some "David" who would try to knock his block off, and Campbell was a lot handsomer than Goliath. Thus it was that a pleasant-natured fellow, honest, an actual "do-gooder" at heart, came to be so handy with his cast-iron fists. Countless times he had found it necessary to end a session of undeserved ill treatment by knocking the daylights out of his oppressor. As all the bullies wised up and kept their distance, the devotees of pugilism stepped in to convince the "Oregon Giant" that he was a natural and that it would be a waste to humanity if he didn't meet the challenges of the prize ring. By the time Dempsey was on the boat from San Francisco, Campbell, too, had the reputation of being unbeaten in the ring.

Dempsey's arrival in Portland was unheralded in the press. He and his companions set up their headquarters at Joe Taylor's Willamette Palace, a large north end saloon with enough room for a twenty-four- by twenty-four-foot ring. Old Joe Taylor was one of the few Portlanders with his money on Dempsey, having been instrumental in bringing him to town. Taylor's saloon was the mecca of Portland pugilism. It was there that Dempsey set up a training schedule and met with reporters and enthusiasts from Pacific Coast cities arriving for the match.

The opinion in Portland was that Campbell was an unbeatable force of nature. A sports editor told how when Dempsey showed up at his office and handed him his card, "I felt sorry for the poor guy." When Dempsey became aware that the people in the newsroom thought he was not up to the task of fist fighting the giant Campbell, he declared, with a confident smile, that he would "unjoint the giant's nose in the third round." Those making size and weight comparisons between the two made the mistake of putting their money on Campbell. In fact, the people of Oregon were putting their money almost exclusively on Campbell. The same could not be said for the handful of enthusiasts from San Francisco and Seattle. They had seen the lightning fists and dancing maneuvers of the Nonpareil, and they were not expecting to go home broke—even though they had put every penny they could muster on the fight. According to Richard Fox, "Their coin, watches, rings, studs, cuff-buttons, etc., had found resting places in the pool boxes, and thousands of dollars of Campbell money went floating about which they were unable to cover, as galling as it did seem."[28]

## PORTLAND'S FIGHT OF THE CENTURY

The upcoming fight would be one that the spectators would talk about for the rest of their lives and that the sportswriters of the twentieth century would relate to readers long after the participants were dead and gone. This fight would be Queensberry ring rules, but because it was a prizefight, without the limited rounds permitted in the city, it meant that it would have to be carried out as an "excursion." With the publicity, no one in authority would be caught off guard. The police kept an eye on activities, and by the evening of November 2, the news had spread far and wide that the match was underway. As midnight neared, once again groups of men migrated through the darkness under a steady, light drizzle of rain to the ferry docks. By 1:00 a.m., most of the downtown docks were crowded with excursion boats. The steamboat *A.A. McCully* had been procured by Joe Taylor for Dempsey and his nearly two hundred supporters. The larger, more luxurious steamboat *Fleetwood* was filled with Campbell supporters and "champagne friends," such as U.S. senator Jonathan Bourne. There, the mood was quite festive, the deck alight with glowing cigars and the air crackling with laughter.

Lining the docks as far down as the Stark Street Ferry landing were even more steamboats: the *City of Salem*, the *New York*, the *City of Sellwood* and the *Calliope*. At two o'clock, the *A.A. McCully* shot a short blast of white steam into the night air, signaling that it was moving out. By then, the drizzle had turned to rain.

Johnny Regan. *From Richard K. Fox,* Life and Battles of Jack Dempsey, *1889.*

There were no drawbridges to open in those days, so the line of steamboats moved swiftly downstream in a nighttime parade, followed by about "twenty other craft of cheaper rate excursionists." This must have been a strange sight for any night watchman, staggering drunkard or footpad awake at this hour. The armada steamed down the ship channel on the downstream starboard side of Swan Island, beneath the high cliffs of Mocks Crest, past Saint Johns and out past the channel lights into the wide Columbia River.

There, the armada was met by a small steamboat bearing several authorities, sheriffs and the like from Clark and Cowlitz Counties. The officials on board made it clear that any prizefighting on their jurisdictions would bring arrests and stiff penalties for all involved—including the esteemed Joseph Taylor. The gentlemen in the armada politely thanked the lawmen for their gracious advice and, with great blasts of steam, moved down the swift-flowing waters of the Columbia. The lawmen, having done their civic duty, went home to their warm, dry beds, most likely thinking that no prizefight could be successful in such a cold, driving rain.

Undeterred, the line of boats moved downstream some twenty-five miles to the mouth of the Lewis River. Here, there were no authorities waiting to ambush them. Here, they were joined by the steamboat *Clara Parker* from Astoria, with about one hundred passengers, followed by rowboats and other small craft from the towns on the Oregon side of the Columbia—Saint Helens and Columbia City.[29]

A short distance from the mouth of the Lewis River, they came to low banks and a sand bar that indicated the end of the line. Here was a broad, newly mown field belonging to Joseph Sprecht, who, by arrangement, had agreed to allow the contest to take place on his land. Shortly past dawn, the rain lightened, and some of the men went to arrange the ring, although the farmer had forgotten to bring over a wagonload of sawdust, as requested. Before hopes could rise concerning the weather, the cisterns in the sky opened, and a driving rain came upon the land, lasting for hours without letting up. The men aboard the steamboats had to turn their attention to snoozing, or cards or polite conversation, making sure their companions stayed awake. Many a cigar was smoked, coffee guzzled by the quart, sandwiches eaten and games of whist won and lost until the rain turned to mist—or, better yet, the sky cleared.

# 5

# Near the Mouth of the Lewis River[30]

Along the river was a line of nearly every size of craft. Some folks who had come in rowboats huddled together under an overhang of cottonwood roots made by a washed-out embankment. With the smoke from roaring fires here and there and the steam from idling steamboats, the gathering of men had taken on the air of an army encampment. It seemed to be an all-male affair (although there were reports of at least one girl dressed as a boy). Men had come by horseback and on foot from nearby farms, and together with the river travelers, the audience came to about one thousand, many of whom had never before witnessed a prizefight.

As noontime came with a weak November sun barely visible behind the clouds, the champions finally showed their faces, and all seemed ready to begin. Then everyone was driven suddenly from the battlefield by a burst of rain. The rain pounded down for another half hour before the clouds broke apart, even revealing a bit of pale blue. This time, the fight would go on.

The crowd that remained in the comfort of the steamboats had their enthusiasm restored by seeing the fighters walking together toward the gathering of umbrellas where the ring was located. As was the pugilist tradition, this was the time for the crowd to choose a referee. By acclamation, Captain James Carroll was chosen as referee. Carroll was the captain of the Alaska steamer *Ancon* and was well liked up and down the coast. Among his many talents, he was admired for his knowledge of applying the rules of the ring. James Georghan and B. Fitzgerald were the timekeepers, men well known to the crowd who frequented the Willamette Palace or some of the north end oyster bars with room for a ring.

Dempsey was seconded by his friends and fellow pugilists Jack Keenan and Tom Cleary, while Campbell was seconded by the oversized Scotsman Duncan McDonald and Dick McCarron, a young tough from Astoria. At 12:30 p.m., the contestants stripped off their outer garments, both displaying remarkable physiques. At 12:40 p.m., time was called, and according to Richard K. Fox of the *National Police Gazette*, Campbell jumped into the ring holding a wad of bills and called out, "I'll bet $500 that I win."[31] Dempsey's supporters could only grit their teeth and smile, having already bet every dime they owned on their champion.

Dave Campbell entered the contest with the confidence of a young, unbeaten giant. He went for Dempsey with his powerful left thrust, but Dempsey never seemed to be in the same place he had been a fraction of a second earlier. He dodged Campbell's giant fists for a while, though Campbell got in a jab to his ribs. This caused Dempsey to slip on the wet grass, briefly going down on his knees. He rose with a fury and tore into Campbell, who gave back as much as he was given. The round ended as the contestants were bound in one of those hugging clinches that are often seen in fights.

Even though the rounds were under Queensberry rules, they seemed to fly past. The second round brought what the audience had come to see: fast, expert sparring between two giants of the ring. Dempsey, much smaller than Campbell, was adept at avoiding contact but received a painful blow to his shoulder, while Dempsey landed a blow squarely on Campbell's cheek that would have sent him flying had it been directly on the nose. There was some more tit for tat and the second round was over.

In the rest between rounds, it is said by those near the Campbell corner that Campbell said to his seconds, "I'll finish him up in the next round." The third round came with the two fighters cautiously circling, having been made aware of their opponent's strong suits by painful bruising. The suspense of such encounters is very strong and may be one of the dark pleasures the pugilistic follower seeks in watching such sport. Finally, Campbell pounced with a terrible blow that would have done damage had it hit the target—a target that seemed to appear and disappear, popping up out of nowhere and falling back again. The power of his blow caused Campbell to slip a little on the soggy hay. What happened next is best taken verbatim from a firsthand report:

> *The next instant he lay prostrate on his back, having fallen as if shot through the heart. It was a great surprise to everybody. Campbell lay in the center of the ring, apparently unconscious. Slowly he turned himself over, and finally he got up on his hands and knees, but by this time more than 10 seconds had elapsed, and the Oregon champion was knocked out.*

The move had been so rapid that very few observers saw how it was done. If they had been attentive, they saw Dempsey lay a blow on Campbell's chest as he was recovering—a blow that seemed too weak to have done any damage. What they didn't see was the quick thrust of a left jab to the side of Campbell's nose. The blow broke the nose, and Campbell was knocked unconscious. Later, it was decided that Campbell's nose could be straightened, but his big fight was lost.

Some of the members of the press had come down aboard the *City of Salem*, bringing with them cases of type and some of their better "lightning compositors" (or type-throwers), as the typesetters of the day were called. The reporters working for papers wishing to print an "extra" edition with particulars of the fight got to work writing something the type-throwers could have ready upon the return of the steamboat. They did this even as the crowd readied itself for the next fight—a bare-fisted contest between Larry Sullivan, a favorite of Astoria, and an up-and-coming talent, Tom Ward from Portland. Both men were sailors' boardinghouse runners (a profession often known as "crimping" or "shanghaiing") who often found themselves in competition in "shipping landlubbers."

Most of the people here did not do so well in their attendance at Sunday school. The Astoria boys were known for their rough edges. It was a town of losers who had gone west because there was no place else for them to go. It was also a town of vultures that fed on the losers, with six or eight saloons on every block and bawdy houses between each one. It was also a good place to change professions. All one had to do was spend a little time in the watering holes down by the canneries and sooner or later he would end up aboard ship, with a new name and a new (albeit poorly paid) profession.

Dempsey had run off to the *A.A. McCully* for a quick wash and a change of clothes—including a warm overcoat. He had been asked to be Larry Sullivan's second, and though the two were as different as two persons can be, Dempsey agreed. He had an affinity for the doe-eyed young man with Irish roots and a connection to the great John L. Sullivan. Matt Dee, a man who shared the same profession as Sullivan, was also in his corner.

The match was prolonged and painful—conducted according to London prize ring rules, with short rounds and even shorter rests. Most of the crowd was ready for it to be over about a half hour into the match. London rules were considered far more barbaric, but on top of that, each of the two men would have been happy to have torn the limbs off of his opponent or, as was Sullivan's forte, gouged his eyes out. From the beginning, "Foul!" was cried throughout by both sides. It was difficult for the referee to catch all the illegal moves and fouls.

After the match had been going for over an hour, Sullivan started to wind down—with blood covering most of his upper torso. Each instance that "Time!" was called after one more short round, Dempsey could be seen at Sullivan's ear, encouraging him, challenging him and giving sage advice. As the rounds wore on, some of the crowd moved away in disgust. After each round, Sullivan would stagger like a dying, bullet-ridden soldier, smeared with blood and earth. His large brown eyes were bloodshot and surrounded by purple bruises; blood dripped from his nose and from his mouth where some teeth had been loosened. Sullivan would drop like a dead weight into his corner, yet when "Time!" was called again, he would rise up like a monstrous corpse under the power of a necromancer. In this case, Dempsey was the necromancer.

At about the hour and a quarter since the fight began, Dempsey found that there was no more water to wash the blood and muck off of his ward. The referee told Dempsey to use mud, and the fight continued. By this time, Sullivan was so far gone with exhaustion and pain that he found it hard to rise and walk to the center of the ring. The referee chastened him, shouting out that he would give the match to Ward if Sullivan didn't come all the way to the center. It seems a twelve-foot walk is a long and hard one for someone who has been pounded with powerful fists for over an hour. Sullivan staggered to the center, where Ward was waiting, giving Sullivan two hard blows to the face. Then the fighters were in a clinch, and Sullivan's stubby fingers made their way to Ward's eye sockets in an attempt to do Ward some real damage. "Foul!" was cried again, this time by the referee, and the match was given to Ward.

The match had lasted about an hour and a half, seventy-seven prize ring rounds, and was one of the most disgusting spectacles ever witnessed by many of the excursionists, who said as much or more as they filtered down to the awaiting vessels. The horses plodded home with their tired and rain-drenched riders, and the rowboats slid across the wide waters of the Columbia, some of them taking advantage of a strong cross wind by putting up sails.

Long before this, even before the Ward-Sullivan fight was brought to a close, the *City of Salem* had headed back upstream with the "lightning compositors" busily putting the reporter's work into a form that could be printed shortly after arrival at the steamboat dock. That evening, there would be extra editions of some of the papers, the demand being an indication of how a great many people in Portland were becoming boxing fans of one sort or the other.

The return trip aboard the *A.A. McCully* with Joe Taylor's crowd, the out-of-town reporters and the rest of the San Francisco crowd was one of exalted celebration. Every man aboard had made a killing on the fight. The other steamboats plodded home under a cloud of disappointment, but gamblers are eternal optimists when it comes to believing that they will make all their money back a hundredfold tomorrow. Dave Campbell had lost every penny he owned, but his luck would change for the better.

It was reported in a later article that in the middle of the celebrations on the homeward journey, Jack Dempsey stood up and declared, "Come on, boys. Campbell is a game man, and now he is broke. Let's give him a good sendoff."

He then took off his derby hat, threw in some gold coins and passed it around to all the passengers on board. Soon, the hat was filled with a small fortune in gold and silver. When Dempsey met up with Campbell, he gave him the hat full of money with the words, "There you are, Dave. That's more than I made out of the fight, so you come out best after all."

It is likely that this story is true.[32] One of Dempsey's most remarked-on qualities was his generosity.

When the armada of steamboats arrived at the ferry docks in downtown Portland, they were met by a jubilant crowd ready to hail Dave Campbell as conqueror. As it was reported in *Pearson's Magazine*:

> *The fire department boys had drawn out all the apparatus available and had festooned with flowers the hose carts and the hook and ladder trucks. In addition, they had hired a barouche which was decked with flowers and drawn by four white horses. In this they intended to parade their hero through the streets.*
>
> *Campbell saw the outfit and hid below the deck. Dempsey's friends from California, who had made some money betting on him, engaged the barouche as it stood and promptly placed Dempsey in it. They thereupon drove to a hotel and celebrated.*[33]

6

# 1886: A Year with No Equal

Portland can have an enchanting effect on some people. The first settlers came because it was a pleasant meadow—a place that seemed like it could be cultivated into a pleasant shire surrounded by friendly hills. In the 1880s, the view from Portland Heights eastward would have been one of pastoral beauty leading up to a sheer skyline of ancient forests on glaciated slopes. Of course, there were the months of endless rain, and when the rain let up, the sky would darken with the billows of smoke rising from cordwood-powered sawmills along the river combined with the fumes of other smoke-belching industry.

Dempsey arrived in Portland not long after transcontinental railroads made Portland a railroad hub. People began to move about with greater and greater ease and in growing numbers. Americans are a people who have the "pursuit of happiness" built into their imagination. It sets them in motion, packing suitcases, dreaming and making plans. Dempsey's plan was to become the greatest champion of all time and then to settle down with a comfortable little tavern like a respectable retired pugilist.

He had been in Portland for several weeks before his contest with Campbell, and it is apparent that the place and the people were agreeable to him. His place of choice for taking exercise and sparring with partners was City Park (now Washington Park), with a panoramic view of Portland and the surrounding mountain ranges—visibility permitting. He also remained in Portland for several weeks following the match; a few nights after the match, he joined Dave Campbell and others in a "glove contest" at the New Market

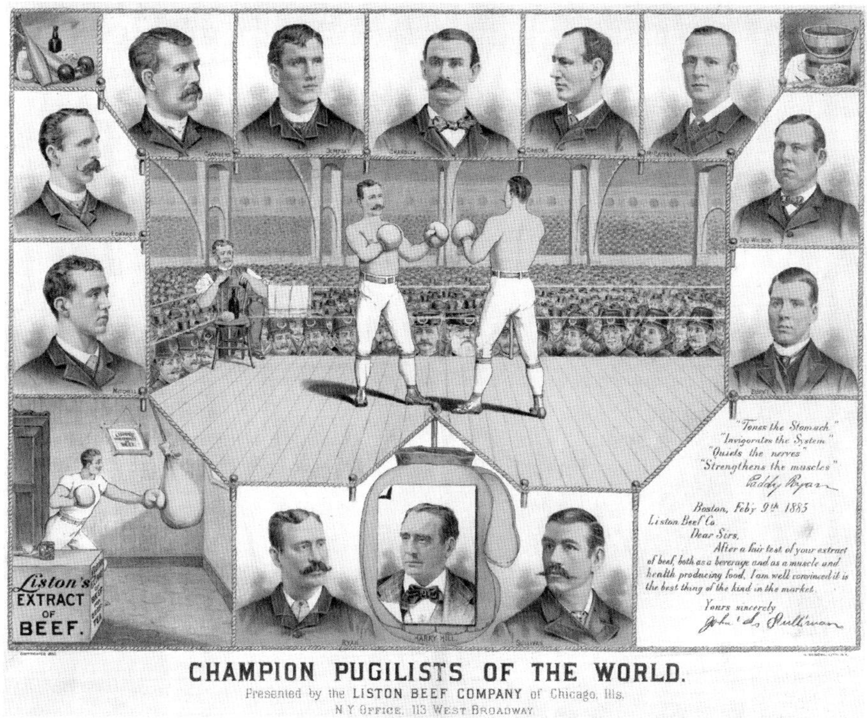


Jack Dempsey. *From a Champion Pugilists of the World poster, lithograph by H. Bencke, 1885, Library of Congress, LC-DIG-pga-00188.*

Theater. Dempsey made friends easily and was a favorite of Joe Taylor, the closest thing Portland had to a boxing promoter. He soon became a favorite of Portland's "sporting class and a very good friend of Dave Campbell."

Not everyone was pleased with the "prizefighting city" reputation that Portland was getting. The day following the Dempsey-Campbell fight, two Portland police officers were suspended by city council for having been a part of the crowd that witnessed the event.[34] These were the sacrificial lambs offered up to that vocal majority of the public who were appalled at the thought of grown men hitting each other with fists.

The week following, a more serious repercussion occurred: Oregon state senator T.T. Geer introduced a tersely worded bill in the state legislature intended to suppress prizefighting by filling in the loopholes that the promoters had been using in the present law. It was an easy job of plagiarism for Geer. Prizefights had been taking place for decades in other states, and other states had found ways to write tougher and tighter laws. Now it was time for Oregon to follow suit. The bill passed with little or no opposition.

At the same time in Washington Territory, the legislature passed a similar bill. The solemn members of that august body were told how the territory was set to become a "pugilistic paradise," with descriptions of the battles waged on the north shores of the Columbia River. They were also given the news that a match was being arranged that would be of worldwide interest: large purses were being arranged to persuade John L. Sullivan to meet black heavyweight Peter Jackson (to believe this would be to ignore Sullivan's racist vow that he would never fight a black man).

It was during this first visit to Portland that Jack Dempsey met the girl who would make certain he returned to Portland. Her name was Miss Maggie Brady, and she had everything a good Irish boy could possibly desire: beauty, modesty and sweetness. I would suggest that it is most likely that Dempsey met this young lady at a social function held in her family parish, Saint Francis Church (on Twelfth Street in what was then East Portland). The likelihood of such a girl in that day, from a religious and respectable family, meeting someone like Jack anywhere else is almost nil. No doubt she was smitten by the very handsome youth, who may have even forgotten (at first meeting) to mention he was a prizefighter. Maggie's father, James F. Brady, was a master blacksmith for the Union Pacific Railroad in East Portland. The family home was a large frame house near the rail shops, and the residents included a grown brother who was a Union Pacific machinist.

The story of the love between the Nonpareil and the Portland girl is one to which reporters gave scant thought. Dempsey was only interesting as a prizefighter, and as far as the press of the late nineteenth century was concerned, a sports figure's love life was his business—unless one of the lovebirds started shooting at the other one. Besides this, Dempsey kept his private life out of the limelight as far as possible. That means there are no known written records of how the events unfolded, but there is evidence that the Brady family was never pleased with Dempsey's profession, even after he was an accepted and loved member of the family.

A champion on the brink of being one of the greatest prizefighters in history had to be about his business. So Jack left the City of Roses, though his heart remained behind. During the first weeks of December 1885, Dempsey saw as much of Maggie as time allowed. He also saw a good deal of Dave Campbell, sparring together in and out of the "glove contest" ring. It was clear to Dempsey that Campbell was a naturally talented boxer—powerful, smart and nimble. Since such a talent would be wasted in the forests and valleys of Oregon, Campbell saw that hooking up with the backers, promoters and managers known to his friend Jack could do him a lot of good. Both men were very young—they seemed to have no illusions that this prizefighting lark was to be their lifelong vocation, but it was a great way for the right person to make money and fame—"making hay while the sun shines," as the expression goes.

## DEMPSEY AND CAMPBELL TAKE OFF

On December 18, Jack Dempsey, Dave Campbell and pugilist Tom Cleary left Portland traveling north and then east to Saint Paul on the Northern Pacific. From there, they would go on to New York City. Traveling with them was the well-known journalist Edgar W. "Bill" Nye. He wrote a syndicated article about the trip that appeared in newspapers across the country. Here are a few excerpts:

Journalist Bill Nye traveled with Dempsey and Campbell. *From* Seattle Post-Intelligencer *cartoon, 1890.*

> *We made a grand, triumphant tour across the country together, and I may truthfully state that I never felt so free to say anything I wanted to—to other passengers—as I did at that time. I wish I could afford to take at least one pugilist with me all the time. In traveling about the country lecturing, a good pugilist would be of great assistance.*
>
> *Well, throughout our long journey across the State of Oregon and the Territories of Idaho, Montana and Dakota, and the State of Minnesota, it was one continual ovation. Dempsey had a world-wide reputation, I found, co-extensive with the horizon, as I may say, and bounded only by the zodiac.*
>
> *Mr. Dempsey is not a man who would be picked out as a great man. You might pass by him two or three times without recognizing his eminence, and yet, at a scrapping matinee or swatting recital, he seems to hold his audiences at his own sweet will—also his antagonist. Mr. Dempsey does not crave notoriety. He seems rather to court seclusion. This is characteristic of the man.*[35]

People were often surprised by Jack Dempsey's unassuming appearance. Dave Campbell looked more the part of a champion. Dempsey was said to have dainty hands—almost like a woman's, although powerful—and the knuckles had been broken and healed more than once. Dempsey was straightforward about his ambition to make the most money he could and then retire, and this trip to New York City was a trip straight into the lion's den as far as prizefighting was concerned. In New York, most of the great matches were challenged and arranged within the offices of Richard K. Fox's *National Police Gazette* in Franklin Square, but Dempsey had notified the press that he would fight any man alive, except John L. Sullivan, for $2,500 a side.

In New York, Dempsey started off participating in friendly rounds at athletic clubs where city folk could also get a good look at the Oregon bruiser he had with him. Dempsey was vigilant about his reputation as Nonpareil, as it was his ticket to the large sums needed to set himself up as a married man of business. He had put on enough weight to be considered a middleweight, so that prize was now before him as well. Shortly after his arrival in New York, he read in the *Boston Gazette* that Tom Bogue, the manager for George LaBlanche (sometimes spelled "Le Blanche"), the reigning middleweight champion of the world, had accused Dempsey of being a coward. Dempsey fumed silently for a while and then suddenly left the Rochester House Hotel, where he was staying with Gus Tuthill, his backer, telling him he was going for a shave.

Dempsey was on the Boston Express within the hour; he showed up at the editor's desk that afternoon and requested that he send for Bogue and LaBlanche. The editor was happy to oblige and to have a front-row seat at the powwow ahead. When the two men arrived, Dempsey was still fuming and refused to shake the hand of Bogue, the originator of the insult. The editor reported the following conversation:

> *"I came here to prove myself a game man, and I came alone. I will fight you right away for $1,000 a side."*
>
> *"I can't raise the money," answered Le Blanche.*
>
> *"Then," said Dempsey, "I will fight you for fun. We will go from here in a coach immediately and fight to a finish, with bare knuckles or gloves, in a room or on the turf."*
>
> *"But I want to fight for money when I fight," said Le Blanche. "I am a poor man."*[36]

Dempsey understood poverty and why LaBlanche would want to fight only for money. They shook hands and were seen together later that afternoon in a restaurant "eating beans out of the same plate, which in Boston is the equivalent to touching glasses." It was understood that a fight between them would soon be arranged. LaBlanche was born in Quebec but had recently been discharged from the U.S. Marines. He was a well-built man with a small frame. His round, slightly balding head was set off by a Roman nose, beneath which he wore finely groomed mustaches. He was known to fight dirty, often using moves he had been taught by the English pugilist Jimmy Carroll.

In early February, Gus Tuthill went to Philadelphia to arrange a fight with Jack Fogerty, who claimed the middleweight championship of America. Arthur Chambers, an ex-prizefighter from England who had made a pile of money, now owned a gym and a saloon in Philadelphia. Chambers, best known as the backer of John L. Sullivan, had heard Dempsey's general challenge to anyone alive and thought his boy Fogerty was up to the task. A match was arranged in secret, although secrets of this sort have a way of leaking out. The authorities caught wind of the upcoming match and started keeping a close eye on the men involved. For the privilege of watching the fight, eight prominent Philadelphians put up $250 each. For this they were allowed to bring a friend. Arthur Chambers put up the remaining $500 for Fogerty's side. On Dempsey's side, Jack Dempsey put up $1,000 for himself, Gus Tuthill put up another $1,000 and a relative, a "Captain" Tuthill, put up the remaining $500. In total, there were no more than four dozen men privileged to attend.[37]

Fogerty had been under the autocratic care of Arthur Chambers, training and working out in a rigorous regimen. Meanwhile, Dempsey had been working out under the supervision of Tom Cleary, the prizefighter from California who had been with him for some time. They had found a reasonable place to train, a ferry ride up the Hudson at Newberg. It wasn't terribly convenient, but it was away from the crowds of fans and noses of reporters. One of Dempsey's least favorite things about the profession was what he called the "lionization," meaning fame and adulation.

On the evening of February 2, 1886, there were no cheering crowds at the Fogerty fight, just a couple dozen serious-looking men in business suits watching their investments at work. All that evening, sporting men who had caught wind of a fight were poking around the athletic clubs asking questions—as were the police. The fight, however, was not held in an arena of any size but in a small hall in Upper Manhattan rented for the occasion. At 11:30 p.m., the hall grew silent, and the two fighters entered. Jack Dempsey was wearing his customary blue shorts and white canvas shoes. Around his waist was the handkerchief of variegated browns that were his "colors," the ones no one had yet taken from him. Jack Fogerty looked especially determined in his dark fighting trunks—mustaches twitching like those on a tomcat itching for a fight. The old-time promoter Al Smith was chosen to be the referee. He read the terms of the match, what the prize money would be and that the fight would be with hard gloves, Marquis of Queensberry rules and a fight to the finish.

It was a brutal fight from the first round to the last, with Dempsey drawing blood from his opponent in the first round. Round after round, Fogerty came into the ring to be mauled, knocked about, knocked down and bloodied, but somehow he managed to crawl back in twenty-seven times.

By the final round, Fogerty's poor face looked like uncooked meatloaf. His eyes were swollen to near blindness, and his body was matted with blood. The last round he went at Dempsey with a brave beginning, until those little Irish fists began battering him like tiny cannonballs shot from a cannon. Dempsey worked Fogerty slowly around the ring and into a corner, and then suddenly his left hand shot into the nape of Fogerty's neck. Fogerty fell like timber. He came slowly to his senses, struggled to get up, rose drunkenly to his feet and then collapsed into a quiet heap. As he did not rise when time was called a second time, Arthur Chambers threw up the sponge. The battle that had raged for one hour and fifty-one

Richard K. Fox. *From Richard K. Fox,* Life and Battles of Jack Dempsey, *1889.*

minutes was given to Dempsey, now the middleweight champion of America.

A glow of good fortune continued to follow Jack Dempsey, whether he was stepping into the offices of the *National Police Gazette* in New York to propose a challenge or stepping into the ring. He was also in love, writing letters dutifully each day to his Maggie in Portland. Sometime earlier, the two had arrived at a date for their marriage, which would take place in July back in Portland. When this fact was mentioned to any of Dempsey's cigar-chomping sportsmen pals, the response was inevitably something like: "Too bad, kid, you would have made a great fighter."

Little did they realize that his dream of settling down to raise a family, with enough cash to set up a cozy sports saloon, was no passing fancy. That—combined with Dempsey's ambition to put down every foe, to make the name of Dempsey as immortal as the mountains—was the drive behind his powerful fists. He was on a short rope. He was to be married in July, and he had promised to give up prizefighting. This gave him the next few months to conquer the world.

To compound his difficulty, Dempsey was in love, meaning he was a little out of his mind. He was more impulsive than usual, as could be seen in his sudden disappearance to Boston on account of the article in the papers. He would also disappear into the streets of New York City to walk and think—sometimes in the pouring rain. His thoughts were with the absent object of his affection, and the halo of love gave him a heroic glow, an aura that did not go unnoticed by the adoring press.

In the months ahead, Dempsey's schedule of training and fighting was rigorous and nonstop. Two weeks after defeating Fogerty, Dempsey was pitched against Pete McCoy at the Oakland Avenue Rink in Jersey City.[38] Originally, the fight was planned for Madison Square Garden, but the New York mayor and police chief had proved[39] "a harsh and cruel mother to the gentle art," so another location was needed. McCoy had a sterling reputation as a fighter with great skill and bravery. He was known to have whipped a giant of a man in Butte City, Montana, in a saloon full of the man's friends. He had laid the Goliath out cold in the second round and then walked over to calmly collect his $1,500 prize money from the gaping-mouthed sourdoughs. He was also rumored to have bettered John L. Sullivan while touring with his troupe.

The buzz about the fight created quite a stir, to the degree that crowds of New Yorkers flocked to Jersey on the night of the fight. To get to the rink, New York dwellers had to go on a pilgrimage through the slushy snow, crossing bridges and waiting for horsecars, all the while grumbling that "it should have been held in the Garden." The rink was at its capacity of six thousand long before the match, with throngs of sportsmen filling the benches on the sawdust floor and spilling up into the balconies. The musicians' balcony, which commanded a superior view of the ring, was jammed with what the *Sun* called "the shining stars of sluggerdom, packed away like sardines."[40] There were George LaBlanche ("the Marine"), Barry Hill, Tom Bogue (LaBlanche's backer) and Jim Keegan (John L. Sullivan's backer), with two dozen other sportsmen, aldermen and capitalists, row upon row, holding their bowler hats in their hands and blowing cigar smoke at the ceiling.

The match was permitted to be fought using Queensberry rules limited to six rounds. Each round grew in intensity, with each fighter raining painful blows on his opponent to the glee of the crowd. The first four rounds seemed to belong to Dempsey, especially the fourth round, where McCoy faltered considerably. In the fifth round, McCoy came at Dempsey with a fresh vigor and managed to land a blow to his ear and then his mouth "that made the smile look more cast iron and ghastly than ever. Fire burned in Dempsey's eye—the fire of revenge."[41] In the sixth and final round, the excitement of the crowd grew to a fever pitch. The two men battered each other with nearly equal skill, ducking and swatting, and then Dempsey was knocked into the ropes and the round was over. The men were ready to fight to the finish, but the Jersey City police chief had already made it abundantly clear that he would not countenance such an activity. The judges gave the match to Dempsey, a fact that made McCoy and his supporters disagree, saying it was an obvious draw. However, the reporter for the *Sun* summed the situation up this way:

> *The six rounds went on in about the same way. Each one was a little hotter than the first, and each was full of blows whose strength made the New Jersey Plebs yell with joy, and whose cleverness filled with admiration and delight the wise men from over the river.*
>
> *The most decided advantage was gained by Dempsey in the fourth round. McCoy seemed for a time to be completely used up, and it was expected that he would be knocked out by Dempsey at any moment. Blows were showered like hail on his face and body, and his friends who thought that the judges should have declared the fight at least a draw will change their minds if they reflect on that critical point in McCoy's journey through the six rounds.*[42]

## A FIGHT FOR THE DIAMOND BELT

The following month brought about the fight Dempsey had been itching for, the fight with the Marine LaBlanche. Everyone from the avid sportsman to the overachieving lawman knew that a big fight was in the air—a fight to the finish. It was the big fight of Dempsey's career, sparring for a $3,500 prize and the coveted *National Police Gazette* Diamond Belt signifying the world champion.

The *Police Gazette* Diamond Belt won by Dempsey. *From Richard K. Fox,* Life and Battles of Jack Dempsey, *1889.*

There were rumors and false starts. The morning of March 13, 1886, the day of the fight, it was suddenly called off. Then that night, Dempsey received word to bring two friends and meet "a party of gentlemen" at the docks at the foot of West Twenty-third Street. He sent one of his seconds, a fighter named Gus Tuthill, to investigate. When Tuthill returned with the news that it was on, Dempsey tore off his clothes and began to rub himself down with bay rum in his pre-fight ritual. Soon he was crossing town on the Twenty-third Street streetcar with Gus Tuthill and Tom Cleary.

They were greeted at the dock by a group of New York's boxing elite with whom they boarded the tug *Ocean Queen*, whose home was Atlantic Dock, Brooklyn. The spectators are listed in Fox's book as follows: Joe Cotton, A. Wright Sanford, Mr. Knapp, Dr. Ordway, Jack Thompson, Mr. Leavett, Mr. John Pollock, Al Smith, Dick Roche and a boxing instructor, James O'Neill. Before leaving for the battleground, the *Ocean Queen* ferried along to a wharf on the North River, where the remainder of the guests were taken on board—all counted for about forty men, including twenty-eight members of the New York Racquet Club. These sturdy fellows would take care of any gangland mugs who would interfere with the fight if they couldn't throw it, though the precautions taken were so thorough that neither sheriff nor hooligan was expected to appear on the battlefield.

As the paddle wheels of the tug churned up the sound, darkness fell. The lights of distant harbors and the smoke of a million dinners cooking mixed with the cigar smoke on deck and filled the evening with a mystical air. This was a mythic event, a prize bout the New York papers would declare "The

Greatest on Record." Tension had been building between the two since Dempsey's arrival in New York, but now all was easy. The only sound was the swishing of the paddle wheels, the whooshing of the steam engine and the low mummer of voices from the men.

The fighters were able to doze a little on board, until the sky began to lighten and the *Ocean Queen* pulled gently up to a ramshackle set of pilings that was once a dock. When the tug tied up, the men were informed that this was a place near the township of Rye, on the border between New York and Connecticut. By 7:00 a.m., the ring had been set up, and the gladiators stepped out before the crowd and stripped to be rubbed down, each according to his custom.

Marine LaBlanche put on a pair of blue tights and dark shoes. It was his tradition to fight with his stockings rolled down, leaving his calves bare. Dempsey wore his standard dark hose and white gaiters. The scales set up on board the *Ocean Queen* showed Dempsey as weighing in at 144½ pounds and LaBlanche at 148¾. By acclamation, Brooklyn alderman John O'Neil was chosen to be the referee.

Two well-dressed gentlemen stepped forward as timekeepers, and one of the "professors" from a New York athletic club stepped forward to make a short speech to the fighters:

> *You will fight according to the Marquis of Queensbury rules, with light gloves; you will break at the call of the referee; make no noise, and go to your corners when either of you knocks the other down and wait until the referee decides whether the fallen man is done up or not. Now then, shake hands.*

There are those people whose superstitions dictate that any break in pre-fight ritual will jinx the fight. These folks would have been highly interested in the fact that the traditional "Maltese cross" that is formed by the gladiators and their seconds before going to their corners before the start failed to form. Tom Bogue of Boston, one of LaBlanche's seconds, was unable to reach the outstretched hand of Tom Cleary, Dempsey's first second. Tuthill was Dempsey's number two, and Patsey Sheppard was number two for LaBlanche.

The men went to their different corners, donned their light gloves and waited for the referee's call: "Are you ready? Time!"[43]

What followed was described in the newspapers as "thirteen desperate rounds bitterly contested…a better and more manfully fought fight was

Robert Fitzsimmons. *From Napoleon Sarony, N.Y.C., 1894, Library of Congress, LC-USZ62-57869.*

never witnessed." The Marine was a formidable opponent for the Nonpareil, wiry, muscular and quick. Although he was not a handsome man, having a pronounced nose, black mustaches and a receding hairline, his body was a specimen of compact power and strength. Dempsey, on the other hand, was smooth—not at all flabby, just deceptively normal in appearance. Beneath Dempsey's surface were determination and the power of a disciplined mind to perform split-second reactions with skill and courage.

The first rounds brought little damage to either fighter as they danced around each other, testing, probing, looking for a way past the punishing reach of their opponent's fists. In the later rounds, the men went at each other like "two prairie buffalo." The fighting was so close and the clinchings so frequent that it was difficult to tell the men apart. Then the blood started to flow, first from an open wound on LaBlanche's left cheek and then from his mouth as Dempsey's fists fell, knocking out two of LaBlanche's teeth. By the eleventh round, Dempsey's fists were described as "visiting the Marine's face like piston rods." By round twelve, it was still impossible to tell who was ahead in the game, with LaBlanche covered in blood and Dempsey covered with bruises and abrasions on his chest and face.

Then followed the fated round thirteen. LaBlanche, bleeding heavily, lurched unsteadily at Dempsey, who was huffing like an exhausted bull. Once more, the men began punishing each other with their fists until the Marine dropped with exhaustion and loss of blood. Time was called, and Dempsey went to his corner. When time was called again, the Marine was unable to rise. As the count ended, he struggled to his feet and, lurching at Dempsey, fell weakly into his opponent's arms. As Dempsey helped the beaten man to his corner, he heard his name being called out as the winner of the *National Police Gazette* Diamond Belt, world middleweight championship.

As soon as the result was called, the crowd began to disperse. LaBlanche was taken to Boston by carriage to have his wounds dressed by a doctor. The nearest telegraph office was accosted by those with ties to the papers, so by the time Dempsey and his supporters arrived at the dock at Hunter's Point, they were greeted by a band of jubilant fans, eager to toast the new world champion. Dempsey, who was never sparing with his hospitality, would foot the bill for drinks as readily as he gave handouts to friends with tales of need. In summing up the event, one reporter noted:

> *It was a notable feature that the most notable men in sporting circles were left out in the cold and did not get the correct tip (as to where and when the fight would be held). Even the old-time sporting news reporters were sent astray after forty-eight hours wild-goose chasing over Long Island and West Chester County. As to the fight, it was a good one, and the gamest any one present had ever witnessed.*[44]

On April 10, 1886, the *National Police Gazette* Diamond Belt was formally presented to Dempsey by Richard K. Fox's representative at Cosmopolitan Hall, New York. The festivities included an exhibition match with Mike Cleary and Jack Fogerty. At that moment, the once poor Irish lad now had every appearance of being at the height of health, wealth and happiness.

Following this honor, Dempsey headed back west, stopping at Philadelphia and Minneapolis to spar with various pugilistic luminaries with his mind set on the final challenge ahead—the last hurdle before settling down to a life of nuptial delights. A fight was planned for May 31 in Chicago, pitting the Nonpareil against the singular world heavyweight champion John L. Sullivan. However, this was a match that was not to be. By the time May rolled around, the political climate in Chicago had turned against pugilistic sports.

## A WEDDING IN EAST PORTLAND

July 24, 1886, was a clear day with high clouds cooled by oceanic air. Over in East Portland, there was a congregation of tramps reported to be camped in a pine grove at Twelfth and C Streets. They had polished off three kegs

Saint Francis in east Portland, the church where Dempsey was married and that later held his funeral. *Postcard. Author's collection.*

of beer the previous afternoon and evening. That night, the poor fellows were awakened by an explosion that put them into a frightened and sober state. The explosion was from a sabotaged gas line in a Chinese laundry several blocks away. Then there was a great commotion of fire wagons and a consternation that followed into the early hours. Finally, the "knights of the open road" managed to get some shuteye. Then the sun broke through the branches, and the day began with the sound of clopping, creaking and rolling as farm wagons headed down the rutted dirt road toward the Stark Street Ferry and the markets of Portland. The tramps were still snoozing when the bells from the nearby high towers of Saint Francis Catholic Church at Eleventh and I Streets (now Eleventh and Stark) began to ring glad tidings to all within the sound of the bells. Someone walking in City Park might look east to see where the sound was coming from. The twin bell towers in East Portland made a prominent uppercase *M* that rose up from the tree-lined streets. To the southeast, the village of East Portland huddled against the wharves—and beyond that, a quilt of green patches, farmland and fallow was soon swallowed by the deep green sea of forest marching down from the glaciers.

Readers of the *Telegram* were surprised that morning to see that champion prizefighter Jack Dempsey was being married that day to an East Portland girl. The publicity had been oddly quiet. There was nothing in the *Oregonian*. Though friends and family were aware of the coming event, the family had been so hesitant to bring up the subject of the groom's profession that it is quite likely that many, if not most, of the family attendees to the wedding were unaware of the connection between John E. Dempsey and pugilism. Maggie had taken her beloved at his word; no more would he break his dear fingers and bloody his precious body battling strong, harmful men. At least, that was what she, and the rest of her family, understood to be the case.

Dempsey had the mind of a family man and the heart of a champion—a champion loved throughout the land. The glow of admiration for Dempsey the champion could be seen in the eyes of nearly every schoolboy involved in schoolyard fisticuffs from the Golden Gate to Brooklyn. Either admiration or envy could be seen in the faces of the nation's cigar-consuming sportsmen. Men had made and lost fortunes on the Nonpareil, and now he was apparently going to lay his colors and his gloves aside while victory was still his, a laurel crown for the duration of his life.

The two men were so different from one another—Jack Dempsey from John E. Dempsey—that there was little comparison. Jack Dempsey, prizefighter, was a strong, habitually graceful and fortunate hero. John E. Dempsey, family man, was weak where other men were strong. He was bad with figures, with money, and he struggled with the fact that his poor education put him at a great disadvantage in the world. Dempsey had done everything in his power to make his wedding day wonderful—even though he had promised to become John E. Dempsey in the years following. He was himself a cradle Roman Catholic, born in the holy land of Ireland. He was intent to enter into marriage in the most forthright way possible. In spite of his profession, he was a man of goodwill and good intentions. He was a rarity to Catholic clergy, who were used to either bourgeois merchants and their wives, who were in constant negotiations with God over their petty concerns, or poor women with large families and husbands, who created little corners of Hades by the use of rotgut whiskey. Dempsey was a refreshing change. He had faith—the sort of faith a Nonpareil with little experience with failure might possess. His personality was joyful (he was in love), kind and generous. Except for the unfortunate fact of his profession, he was the ideal of Catholic manhood. And Maggie, Margaret Brady, was as beautiful, loving, sweet and kind as any woman since the archetype of womanhood gave birth to the man who is God (from a Catholic perspective).

Jack Dempsey was at the pinnacle of his fame, so naturally he had friends aplenty. Rich friends, poor friends, they put on their finest to see the "royal" wedding. The lovely church was filled with flowers—on the altars, adorning the statues, perfuming the incense-laden air. As early guests arrived, it could be discerned from the heavenly sound of the choir warming up that this was going to be some classy affair. It seems, between the likes of a twenty-four-year-old boxer, flush with prize money, and a master machinist, manager of the Union Pacific shops, old Portland could pull off a wedding fit for a governor, a king or a Nonpareil and his bride—the girl with the innocent blue eyes. The wedding was a solemn high-nuptial mass, complete with the sublime music of a full choir well trained in turning Latin vowels into celestial overtones. It was celebrated by Father Louis Verhaag, a Dutch-born lion of a man with a broad face, long white hair and full white beard. His years ministering in the drab mining towns of Idaho had prepared him for nearly anything, so counseling the world Diamond Belt champion toward the married life was all in a day's work. He had told Dempsey that marriage was a form of martyrdom, requiring great sacrifice. It was a fact he repeated in his sermon, a sermon that Dempsey may have interpreted differently than the reverend father intended. Jack was used to spending the money he earned, and after a slew of handouts to needy relatives and friends, numerous victory celebrations and $200 train tickets across the continent, he wasn't as flush as he let on—and now he was taking on the responsibility of being a provider. It was just a few days before the wedding that Dempsey sent this note to the *New York Sun*, which was quoted (or misquoted) around the country in various newspapers:

> *Jack Dempsey writes from Portland, Ore.: "I have so many friends in Portland I have about made up my mind to settle here for good and retire from the prize ring. I should not wonder if before long you should see in the papers that Jack Dempsey had been married to Miss Delia* [sic] *Brady, but I will have to let prize fighting alone, as that will be one of my marital promises."*[45]

Good intentions or not, the fact remains that Jack Dempsey did not really anticipate quitting the prize ring immediately upon entering into his marriage bonds. Less than a month before his wedding, Dempsey had sent a telegram from Portland, Oregon, to the offices of the New York *National Police Gazette* challenging the English champions (at that time taking on challengers in the States) Charley Mitchell and Jack Burke. Scuttlebutt had reached Dempsey's ears, coming from those fighters, that he did not deserve the middleweight Diamond Belt. The telegram reads, in part:

> *Portland, Oregon, June 27th.*
> *I will meet either Burke or Mitchell, with or without gloves, Queensberry or London prize-ring rules, for the Diamond Belt and $5,000 a side...*
> *I am ready to fight any man in America at 154 pounds, for $5,000 a side. A battle can be brought off here, and I am satisfied that Richard K. Fox shall hold the stakes. If any would-be champions mean business let them put up $500 forfeit with the* Police Gazette *and I will have it covered, and quickly make a match to fight in three, four, or five weeks. I mean business, as usual. Yours, Jack Dempsey.*[46]

The words "I mean business, as usual" would have brought a sudden chill to young Maggie's soul if she were to have read them. In Dempsey's mad rush to gather up as many laurels as possible prior to marriage, he had missed a few contenders. For a man of such even temper, he was unusually thin skinned when it came to his reputation as a fighter. He was the Nonpareil, and he intended to stay that way, business as usual—and he intended to do it from the new fighting capital, Portland, Oregon.

There were many good intentions from around the country toward the Nonpareil's new life with his bride. Newspaper reporters across the country replaced their lack of information with speculative fictions about the "proverbial luck of Jack Dempsey." One paper reported that "Dempsey's friends won't let him go into the saloon business; they made him deputy coroner instead." Another rag reported that the Nonpareil was going to use part of his fortune to open a hotel. The more cynical sports reporters knew a few facts—like Dempsey's way of blowing through money, paying for the entertainment of his Brooklyn brethren, bequeathing handouts to needy friends and the undeniable fact that Dempsey had a list of previous arrangements and challenges still hanging in the air.

There are no known records remaining of intimate discourse between Jack Dempsey and Maggie, but it must have been the case that Dempsey was able to charm and persuade his bride into delaying the due date of his marital promise to quit the ring—at least long enough for him to rebuild the family bank account. Dempsey swooped up his bride at the height of his glory, a wave that was still cresting. Now it was time for him to show her the real world—his world. She had been released from a claustrophobic Roman Catholic girlhood by her prince. Dempsey let it drop to the *Oregonian* that they were headed to Clatsop for their honeymoon, and then, on July 27, the couple boarded the train for San Francisco.

## SAN FRANCISCO HONEYMOON

Upon arrival in San Francisco, Dempsey soon found that public opinion had experienced one of those California earthquakes, shifting pugilism's legal status into an unfavorable light. A week or so following their arrival, Dempsey was involved in a prizefight at the Oakland Theater. The event was between Dempsey's coach and companion Tom Cleary and Australian fighter Martin "Buffalo" Costello. Dempsey, Charlie Taylor, Jim Coyle and Pat Carr were the organizers, as well as acting as principals and seconds. Once the first blood appeared, the theater filled with policemen. All the "ring leaders" were arrested under felony indictments, and even many spectators—including an unnamed U.S. senator—were arrested for the misdemeanor charge of attending a prizefight. All this must have been quite exciting for the Catholic schoolgirl from Portland town.

It seems Dempsey had no immediate plans to move to Portland, to "start a hotel" or any other "legitimate" business. He telegraphed a reply to a query from the *New York Sun* stating that he planned to return to New York the following month. It may be that he was convinced that Maggie would love New York, but Portland natives are likely to break out in spots from homesickness if they are transplanted too far from the banks of the Willamette.

While among friends in San Francisco, Dempsey set about trying to arrange a fight with the English champion Jack Burke. Burke had been mouthing off to the newspapers about how Dempsey was going to try to weasel out of fighting him. He was a powerfully built, arrogant youth upon whose mouth Dempsey was itching to plant a fist. The match was tentatively set for the September 27 in San Francisco. The permit, however, was not forthcoming. Elections were rolling around in November, and the mayor was adamant that there would be no more of these so-called glove contests (at least not until after the elections). The permit was finally granted, and the fight was set for November 22 at 7:00 p.m. at the San Francisco Pavilion.

Crowds of excited fans began to line up on Larkin Street in front of the Pavilion at four o'clock in the afternoon. By the time the doors opened, there was such a press of people it took a squad of policemen to keep them from rushing the gate. The Pavilion was filled to beyond its capacity, with seven thousand spectators in attendance. The match was not what either fighter expected. It was announced as being Queensberry rules and ten rounds maximum. The two champions slugged away at each other through all ten rounds, giving it all it was worth, but they seemed so evenly matched that neither one had the advantage.

At the end of round ten, time was called by the timekeeper. Burke left the ring, but Dempsey remained seated while the referees scratched their heads and debated the merits of what they had witnessed. Dempsey was ready to fight on, and apparently Captain Douglas of the police was willing to allow it, but Burke refused, saying the agreement was ten rounds. Following this, the referees came back with the decision that the match was a tie, which would have upset the fans had they not witnessed a true exhibition of fistic science. Years later, speculation would arise that Burke was the actual winner but one of the referees was reluctant to be the one to end Dempsey's unbeatable record—there is no way to know for certain. The two men were both winners, coming away richer and ready to continue a lucrative business. Within a few weeks, the two Irish lads were touring as the "Burke-Dempsey Combination" under the management of Charles E. Davis. This gave Maggie a chance to see such exotic sites as opera houses in Salt Lake City and Chicago.

On December 29, 1886, the *New York Sun* announced, "Jack Dempsey is coming home tomorrow." The writer meant New York, Dempsey's home

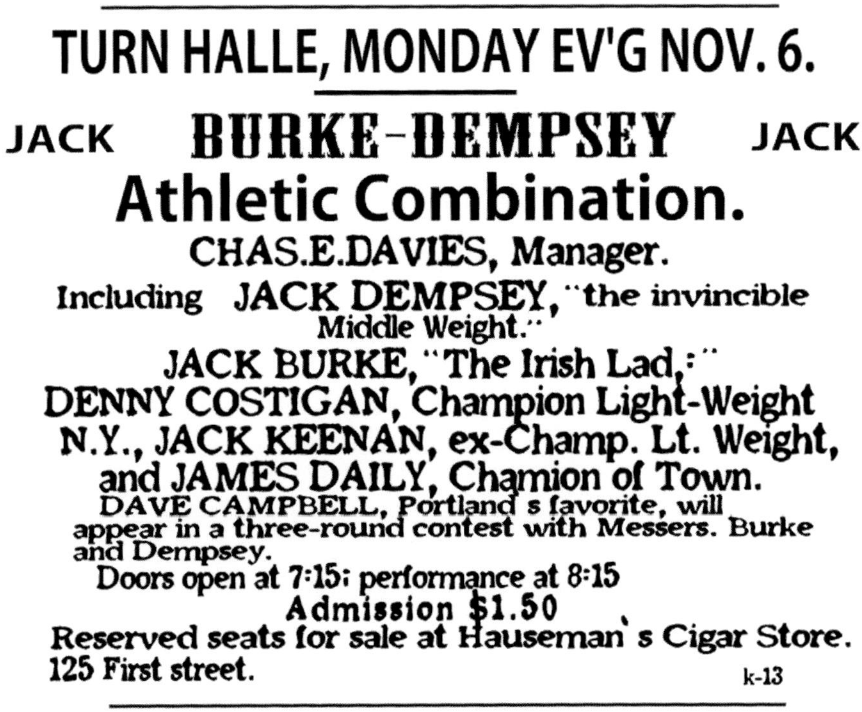


Burke-Dempsey. *Facsimile of an advertisement in the* Morning Oregonian, *November 5, 1886.*

and a city that was proud of its champion. If Maggie had won her husband over to the idea of settling in Portland, Oregon, the New York papers had yet to hear of it. The year 1886 had been a phenomenal one for Jack the Nonpareil, and the latter part was an extended honeymoon for the couple. It also gave Dempsey time to renegotiate his wedding promise, and Maggie, with her pliable and trusting nature, would not stand in the champion's way. She loved him too much to do that. Had Jack Dempsey honored his promise to quit the ring, his name would not be as glorious in the *National Police Gazette* list of champions, but it is possible that his short life as a family man would have been considerably brighter.

# 7
# The Wild Boys of Astoria

Back home, pugilists and pugilist pretenders were coming out of the woodwork across the state, especially in Portland and in its little sister city of Astoria, at the mouth of the Columbia River. There was already a natural rivalry between the two ports. Portland was 113 miles upriver—two undammed rivers with fluctuating currents, channels and sandbars. In the months of the year with low water, Portland shippers and merchants were left with the task of moving cargo onto shallow-bottomed steamboats and barges to and from vessels at anchor in Astoria. For years, the city fathers of Astoria had felt cheated out of being the port city of the Columbia. The wide harbor in the river's mouth could have made Astoria into another San Francisco but for the lack of railroads, merchant houses and banks. For years, the city had tried to get a railroad connecting to the wheat lands of the Willamette Valley and to the other terminals, but to no avail. This meant that all those with business in ships—merchants, boardinghouse runners, ship's agents, crew and so on—were in a constant flux, riding the steamboat ferries back and forth between the two cities in the course of their business. There were no roads to speak of—except for the wretched, muddy wagon tracks that Rudyard Kipling made fun of during his visit to Oregon. Even Portland streets were often unpaved and prone to turning into swamps of mud. Kipling said that they were "worse than that of a poor Irish village." Travel by steamboat, on the other hand, was elegant, comfortable and fast.

Larry Sullivan had risen to the top of the Astoria prizefighters by the extraordinary stamina and violence he had displayed in his fight with Tom

Ward of Portland. Those who recalled the Dempsey-Campbell match often talked more about the second fight. They would recite with awe how in the end, Sullivan, so bruised and covered in blood that he no longer looked human, was gripping Ward with his left while trying to gouge his eyes out with the fingers of his right—a move that cost him the match as a foul. Before the match, Sullivan had thrown so many tantrums that the *Oregonian* had declared he was "without sand," a term that meant something like "guts." No one was saying that now.

Sullivan was a big, pretty boy with large brown eyes, a classic face—like that of an Austrian prince—and a conniving, criminal mind. He also had a temper and a gigantic ego, and was more than inclined to bully the little people of the world, such as you and me. Soon after his arrival in Astoria, he discovered that there was money to be made in providing ships with crews. The crews would nearly always be persuaded by the sailor's boardinghouse runners to desert their vessels. They were promised (after three to five months at sea) great meals, luscious women and a better ship paying more money. This would put them at the mercy of the sailor's boardinghouse, and more often than not, they would leave Astoria sadder and poorer than when they arrived. The ship captains whose crews had deserted would be forced to pay high prices to get them replaced—often with landlubbers and shanghaied fools instead of able seamen.

At first, Sullivan worked as a runner for the infamous James Turk, the father of shanghaiing in the Northwest. Sullivan would work out of either the Turk's boardinghouse in Astoria or the one on Second and C Street in Portland. He was a noticeable character in his swell suit, clean shaven and smelling of Pinaud's Lilac Vegetal, strutting confidently about his illegal and immoral business as though he were a banker. Before long, he had opened a boardinghouse of his own in Astoria. In those days, the businesses were relatively collegial for something that was akin to crime families or criminal gangs. Besides the mighty Turk family, there were several other boardinghouses in the sailor racket—the first being the Grant family, under the guidance of the prim Irish widow Bridget Grant. Another less tidy establishment was the Liverpool House, down by the canneries, run by a muscle-bound lad with an eye toward pugilistic sport by the name of Richard "Dick" McCarron.

Many of the youths who had no qualms about working as runners for the boardinghouses were also prima donna prizefighters. One young man, Matthew Mark Dee (Matt Dee, sometimes Mark or M.M. Dee), had been sent to sea at the age of twelve—not uncommon in those days. He roamed the seven seas for twelve years, during which time he became a first officer. His last voyage, aboard the full-rigged clipper *Jabez Howes*, ended at San Francisco, where he was arrested on a charge of cruelty and assault, brought by a crew member. After being acquitted by the U.S. shipping commissioner, the stocky sailor kicked around San Francisco for a while—renewing an old Tammany acquaintance, the famous Blanche Walsh, an actress of national fame. (In later years, he would brag that he had married her, a fact her biographers may not agree with.)

It is likely that Dee studied boxing with one of the "professors" at one of the popular athletic clubs, and it is further likely that he first came to Portland and Astoria because of the prizefighting, but he found money to be made helping Richard McCarron ship landlubbers.

His first brush with the law in Oregon was when he, along with prizefighter Tom Ward, was arrested by U.S. marshals and brought before Commissioner Lamson in Portland for offenses committed aboard the *Tilley E. Starbuck*. It turns out they had been working for James Turk at the time. Dee would become well known to the authorities wherever he set up shop, which in Astoria was the Liverpool House. He would also become a well-known promoter of pugilistic events in Portland and the proprietor of the Turf Exchange Saloon in Portland—a place with its own prize ring and a telephone connection with the Western Union telegraph office to bring the results of sporting events to gaming customers. He would also find that his temper, invariably linked to his fists, would be a continual source of trouble for him in both police and civil courts.

Throughout the 1880s, "friendly" and unfriendly "glove contests" were held at any venue large enough to assemble a small crowd and dry enough to give the assembly a break from the incessant rain beating down from the North Pacific. The skating rink, Liberty Hall, and later the rooms of the Astoria Athletic Association became the scenes of "glove contests for points" that somehow usually deteriorated into bloody affairs with someone getting knocked cold. Larry Sullivan's name was often on the bill, as was Thomas Warren, styled as "champion of the Pacific Coast." The muscular, sometimes lightweight, sometimes middleweight Albert Johnson of Astoria was always trying to best Tom Ward or any other pugilist who would accept his challenge. He was mimicked in these efforts by a motley assortment of delinquents such as Martin Leonard, James Dyer and Jim McCarron (Richard McCarron's brother). Most, if not all, of these young men would appear on the U.S. marshals' reports as being involved as runners for the local sailor's boardinghouses. Sometimes it took convincing to persuade a landsman that he should join the ranks of the mariners. What better sort of person to do this work than a young aspiring prizefighter?

Portland and Astoria were on a circuit of places where a matchmaker or a rouge prizefighter could come and make challenges with an eye toward making some serious money, not just the fifty-cent bets that could be expected in a barroom—not to say that either city was free from fighting in the bars. Joe Taylor in Portland had set up a full-scale Queensberry rules prize ring in his place in Portland's so-called Whitechapel. In Astoria, a place where the saloons outnumbered the churches twenty to one, where the Finnish fishermen mixed in the saloons with German cannery bosses and Norwegian lumberjacks, the dangerous testosterone levels often exploded into violence. The Finns liked to reach for their *puukkos*, the curved fishing knives usually worn on the belt, whereas the Norwegians and the Irish thought their fists were good enough for any task at hand. The Americans (anyone who was actually born here) would sometimes reach for a revolver—like a Colt Navy—small enough to not hurt the hand with its kickback but large enough to make big holes. In both cities, there was, intertwined with the lower classes of white society, a constant background of Chinese society. These two worlds, joined together in time and space, were constellations apart in essence.

The young white thugs of Astoria were green but dangerous—like seventeen-year-old Jack Grant, son of the infamous Bridget Grant, madam of shanghaiers, with sailor's boardinghouses in both Astoria and Portland. He happened to be in the same saloon as Matt Dee not long after the Irish seaman's arrival in Astoria. Dee was quite naturally soliloquizing on his past achievements with his fists when Jack Grant could no longer stand to listen. The boy was young, his mother had forbidden him to drink and he was feeling the sorts of surging in temper and deadening of reason that accompanies novice attempts at boozing like a man.

Jack had been working as a runner for Larry Sullivan's boardinghouse and was in the habit of cowing sailors. The ex-sailor Matt Dee would not be cowed. No doubt, the twelve years Dee had spent before the mast had taught him a good deal about boardinghouse runners, bullies and novice drinkers. Jack Grant whipped out a twenty-dollar gold piece and challenged Dee to a fight. Dee threw down his twenty-dollar piece to accept the challenge, and as he headed Grant's way, the boy pulled a gun. At that moment, a local tugboat captain named Gage reached over and took the gun away from Grant.

A crowd followed as the two men headed for an empty lot at the edge of town. A referee was chosen, and within a minute or so, the fight was over with a single blow placed by Dee directly in Grant's solar plexus, knocking all the wind out of the doubled-over lad. From that moment on, Jack Grant and Matt Dee were said to be the best of friends—although Dee was twenty dollars richer than before the fight.

By the end of the 1880s, the young punks were mature enough to be a danger to society—especially the society of sailors. Most, if not all, of the sluggers of Astoria worked as sailor's boardinghouse runners at one time or another—a dangerously competitive occupation. They would slug it out with various foes in their line of work (the day job) and then slug it out with one another in the newly formed Astoria Athletic Club. This was a place where the sluggers could follow in the tradition of the Coney Island Athletic Club, the Olympic Club in Chicago, the California Athletic Club in San Francisco or in any of the other clubs trying to rake in the dollars from the dubiously legitimate trade in blood sports.

During the early part of the 1890s, there was an exodus of hoodlums leaving the quiet fishing village of Astoria for the thriving metropolis that Portland was becoming. Larry Sullivan, Peter and Jack Grant, Dick McCarron and a posse of thugs and runners established themselves in an old hotel on Second Street. "A Hotel for Sailors and Farmers" was the cynical inscription above the door. Sullivan continued to look for prizefights until he grew too pudgy to fit into his pugilist's costume. Both Peter and Jack Grant continued to referee matches on into the twentieth century. Matt Dee ran telegraph betting and boxing saloons in Portland's seedy north end before moving to West Seattle, where he opened a gym and ran a private picnicking beach on Alkai Point. The rest of the sluggers and thugs died of drink, were sent to the penitentiary or straightened up and flew right.

# 8

# The Unfamiliar Taste of Defeat

Jack Dempsey may never have moved to Oregon had he not finally met defeat, but then eventual defeat is a given for a prizefighter. It seems highly likely that Dempsey assumed that once his dear Maggie was endeared to the hearts of his Brooklyn family and friends, and they were dear to her, she would consent to living in the comfortable surroundings of New York. There can be little doubt that Dempsey's young bride was warmly received in Brooklyn, as well as in San Francisco and anywhere else she followed her husband. Maggie's sweet and winning personality was a perfect match for the quiet pugilist. As recognition of Maggie's importance, in a showcase at the New York Athletic Club, among the gloves Dempsey used in all of his Queensberry rules victories, there were displayed a pair of white kid gloves, beneath which was an inscription that read, "The gloves worn by Jack Dempsey when he met his first and only defeat by Miss Brady, July 27, 1886."[47]

Until the end of 1889, Dempsey continued undefeated throughout battles against such luminaries as Bill Dacey, Johnny Reagan and Mike Dempsey, to name a few—although he met with a draw in a fight with "Professor" Mike Donovan at the Palace Rink in Williamsburg. Donovan was an old-time fighter and trainer who had developed a grudge against Dempsey over an incident of spiking that occurred during Dempsey's match with Johnny Reagan, a protégé of Donovan's. Dempsey was spiked in the leg and let it be known that he thought Reagan had spiked him intentionally. The "old" man, then forty-one, had mentioned to some other boxers that he would be

Jack Dempsey. *From Richard K. Fox,* Life and Battles of Jack Dempsey, *1889.*

willing to spar with Dempsey. This sporting tidbit was repeated in the press. When Dempsey heard this, he said something to the effect of: "What! That old-timer? I will lick him with a single punch."[48]

Donovan wrote a full account of the fight in his autobiographical book detailing his years as a pugilist, trainer and boxing instructor at the Teddy Roosevelt White House. This delightful and somewhat self-aggrandizing book also included the full newspaper account of the fight under the headline: "Dempsey Only Draws in Six Round Battle with Donovan—The 'Professor' Surprises His Friends and the 'Nonpareil' as Well."

It was Donovan's contention that the game was made a draw by the referees so as to not ruin Dempsey's run at being unbeatable. Although this was not a defeat, per se, Dempsey must have been rattled by the way the formerly adoring press was of the same mind as Donovan. The article released on the nation's newswires read:

> *Referee O'Brian gave his decision, making it a draw, but in the canvass of over fifty men, with few exceptions, all declared that Donovan should have had the decision, and those who thought otherwise gave Dempsey only a shade of preference on the ground that Dempsey's blows were the heaviest.*[49]

A small setback like this was not the sort of thing to derail his reputation, and his name was still greatest among fighters—with the exception of the giant John L. Sullivan. In January, he even joined his old friend Billy Madden—a man of many talents—in his play at the Poole Theater in New York. The play was a silly farce, complete with a Simon Legree sort of villain, and was called *Around New York*.[50] Naturally, the heroine is rescued by a heroic pugilist—in this case, Billy Madden. Audiences were delighted by it, and I am sure it made a nice break for Maggie from tending the wounds of her prizefighter husband.

## THE PIVOT PUNCH FROM THE BLUE

On the morning of April 26, 1889, Jack Dempsey, along with his wife and their new baby girl, arrived in East Portland aboard the *Southern Pacific* after a seven-day journey from New York. With them was Dempsey's trainer, Denny Costigan. It had been two and a half years since Maggie had seen her parents, now also the grandparents of her daughter. There was a reception for the couple at the Brady house in East Portland, next to the Union Pacific machine shops. The reunion would not be for long. Dempsey and Costigan were off the next day for San Francisco, but this time Jack didn't have the heart to wrench his wife out of the arms of her family again. It would be the first time they were apart since they were married. This trip was to renew old friendships at the California Club and to work out the details of responding to a challenge from Dempsey's old nemesis, the "Marine" George LaBlanche. The Marine had a way of irritating Dempsey with his bravado and persistence in challenging the champion. It was said, however, that LaBlanche wasn't the same fighter as Dempsey had met earlier—he was tougher, more "scientific" with his fists and less of a hothead. Experts like Richard K. Fox thought it unlikely that LaBlanche would win, but the fame of the contestants was bound to make it a success, even though there was no belt at stake. The prize, however, was worth slogging for—a substantial $5,500, with $500 to be granted the loser.

The date of the bout was set for August 22, 1889, at the new quarters of the California Club exhibition hall—the old San Francisco armory, a venue with room for over one thousand spectators. In the weeks leading up to the ordeal, Dempsey spent as much time in Portland as he could, though the better sparring partners and trainers could be found in San Francisco. Several days before the bout, Dempsey went down on the *Southern Pacific* accompanied by Dave Campbell. After arrival, Campbell wrote to a friend in Astoria[51] stating that "the general impression in this city is that Dempsey will hang the marine's scalp to his belt" and that there was very little betting going on. This was in spite of the fact that the Marine outweighed Dempsey by over twenty pounds. LaBlanche was unable to meet the weight requirements to challenge the champion for his middleweight prize belt.

The fight, when it took place, seemed to take place more in the eye of the beholder than in reality, as the reports varied wildly from one another. Eyewitness reports in the newspapers tended toward the opinion that Dempsey was punishing LaBlanche severely from the get-go. The crowd was heavily in favor of Dempsey, hissing when the Marine made points. In the seventh round, a gleeful cry of "First blood!" went up as Dempsey landed a blow that brought blood spurting from LaBlanche's mouth. Not only did this count as points, but it was also a common practice of sportsmen to wager on which fighter would be the first to draw blood.

The three-minute Queensberry rounds flew past in a match that all present would retell, and embellish on, for the rest of their days. The men seemed closely matched, and the rounds rolled on with "science" and surprises aplenty. During the twenty-second round, LaBlanche performed what seemed like a conjuring trick, pirouetting 360 degrees on his heel with an outstretched right—a move Dempsey avoided. Just before the gong rang for the end of the twenty-ninth round, Dempsey landed a blow to LaBlanche's face that caused him to slip to the floor. The next round, Dempsey was able to work the Marine's face over some more, though it seemed not to faze him. By this time, the spectators were anticipating that the slugging match belonged to Dempsey, though—barring a knockout—it would be close.

The thirty-first round started to look bad for the Marine. Dempsey drove him into a corner and began hammering with both fists. LaBlanche stoutly resisted. He feigned a weak blow at Dempsey—as though he were growing tired—and then deftly retreated from the counter blow while executing another of his whirling pivots with a ridged right arm. The bare wrist of the gloved hand landed squarely on Dempsey's nose with the power of a wrecking ball. The blow must have broken Dempsey's nose, but he was knocked flat on his face, adding further injury to the insulted nose. It happened so fast that many of the spectators cheered, thinking it was the Marine face down on the mat. Then came the horrid realization: the Nonpareil was out, and many of the sportsmen were out the money they had wagered.

The knockout blow was a dirty trick the Marine was said to have learned from his trainer, English pugilist Jimmy Carroll. The move had never been used in a prizefight and would never again be used, as it was ruled illegal from that time forward.

## JACK DEMPSEY WEPT

Most newspapers reported that Dempsey was "put to sleep" in the thirty-first round, a tidbit that has become a part of boxing history. This was not the view of Jack Dempsey or of many of the eyewitnesses to the battle who tell a different tale. Journalist Henry E. Reed had a front-row seat behind Dempsey's corner, where he sat with pugilist James J. Corbett. The match was not long underway before Corbett remarked to Reed, "He's not the old Dempsey."[52] John L. Herget, better known in the prize ring as "Young Mitchell," was another ringside spectator. He described the punch in this manner: "It was a swing you could use a thousand times and never hit with it. It was ruled out because when the blow did land it wasn't with one's fist."[53] The *Oregonian* reporter who was eyewitness to the fiasco stated, "The Nonpareil was up in seven seconds, but referee Cook had counted him out, and he was a whipped man."[54]

As Dempsey was consoled in his dressing room by Young Mitchell, Dave Campbell and the unnamed reporter from Portland, he wept bitterly over the ordeal. The chances of LaBlanche agreeing to another match now that he had done his damage were slim to nil. As Dempsey

Jack Dempsey, formal photograph. *Author's collection.*

stepped out into the late night chill, the crowd that still lingered in the street sent up a cheer. LaBlanche didn't fare so well. He was sent away with a cold shoulder, and some hoodlums with misguided loyalty pelted his hansom cab with stones.

## THE ROAD TO AN ELUSIVE HOME

At this time in Dempsey's life, he was torn between his old home of Brooklyn, New York, and the lovely little city where his wife, Maggie, and little daughters, Alice and Anne Margaret, were waiting. He was also under contract with the California Athletic Club, from which he needed permission to fight or arrange matches if he were to move to Oregon. His promise to his bride was not forgotten, least of all by members of the press, who were not above mentioning it on occasion.

Following his bout with the Marine, the venues in the major prizefighting cities began to bid for a chance to pit Dempsey against the cream of the Australian fighters who had been invading the States like a new outbreak of "Sydney Ducks."[55] The most outstanding among them was the lanky Bob Fitzsimmons.[56] It was finally agreed upon by both fighters that the Olympic Athletic Club of New Orleans would be the arena. This was after Fitzsimmons stated flatly that he would consider fighting nowhere else, and the club offered Dempsey $12,000 for the bout. Dempsey's main requirement was that no man weigh over 154 pounds stepping from the scales to the ring. By this time, Fitzsimmons had already started to get under Dempsey's skin by signing his name: "Coming middle-weight champion of the world."[57] The date of the match was fixed for January 14 in New Orleans.

Christmastime in 1890 saw Jack Dempsey training in Galveston, Texas, in preparation to meet Fitzsimmons the following month in New Orleans. The North American continent was finally linked by tens of thousands of miles of railroad, but it was not feasible to lay aside one's training and flit between the Gulf of Mexico and the Pacific Northwest for an occasion as sentimental as the Christmas feast.

## DOWNFALL

The evening on which the Dempsey and Fitzsimmons battle was to take place, a great crowd gathered in front of the Olympic Club arena on Royal Street. The venue had a capacity of four thousand spectators, many of whom arrived hours early in order to secure the seats with the best advantage. Dempsey had, as yet, never laid eyes on his opponent. He must have known the "Australian" (as the newspapers called him) was a full four inches taller and was normally thirty pounds heavier, but the full realization of these facts was about to hit home.

It was 9:28 p.m. when the gong rang out for the battle to begin, a fight that was Fitzsimmons's from round one. The lanky warrior's arms were so long that Dempsey had a tremendously difficult time landing a punch. During the third round, Dempsey was knocked down—briefly—and when he rose to his feet, he was groggy.

The punishment continued mercilessly, with the men rushing, ducking, clinching and walloping and Fitzsimmons making the most out of each short Queensberry round. In the seventh round, Fitzsimmons landed a hard blow while the scrappers were in a clinch, giving rise to shouts of "Foul!" The blow seemed to have injured Dempsey, although the referee either didn't see it or didn't call it.

Jimmy Carroll, cigarette card. *Author's collection.*

Toward the ninth round, Dempsey was visibly

weakened, missing blows and receiving blows to the stomach, face and neck. The tenth round saw Dempsey struggle, as though Fitzsimmons were beyond reach, while Fitzsimmons laid Dempsey down for six seconds with a double blow to the stomach. By now, the match was more than won by the "Australian," and many of the spectators were leaving the arena rather than watch the bitterness of the defeat. Fitzsimmons was tired of hitting Dempsey and asked him to throw in the towel. The request was flatly refused. From then until the end, Dempsey was knocked down repeatedly by his reluctant opponent. At the end of a disheartening round twelve, Jack McAulliffe, Dempsey's second, stepped into the ring and begged Dempsey to quit. The argument between the two was still in progress when time was called.

In the thirteenth and final round, Jack was too weak to stop the beating. He was knocked down again but struggled to his feet, whereupon he staggered about the ring in a punch-drunk stupor. In this condition, Fitzsimmons was able to toss a light but merciful blow to his chin, sending him spinning to the floor. The "extra" edition of the *New York Evening World* devoted to the fight gave this colorful account to the end:

> *Fitzsimmons standing over him ready to deliver the final punch said, "Quit, Jack, I don't want to hurt you anymore!"*
>
> *"I'm as good as a dozen whipped men," was the answer, but Dempsey was beaten.*
>
> *There remained, however, a faint hope. "Now look out," cried Fitz, and he swung his right landing carefully and the blow caught Dempsey just below the left ear. He fell to the floor insensible.*
>
> *Carrol twined his arms around Fitz's neck and kissed him, while the latter remarked: "Well, Jimmy, we won't starve this Winter."*
>
> *A hundred men counted the seconds, and when ten was reached Jack was still on his back.*
>
> *"Fitzsimmons wins," shouted the referee.*
>
> *Then a wild cheer went up for the winner. Jack was carried to his corner by McAuliffe, and when his senses returned half a minute later, he wept like a child. Big, burly men, whose tear-buckets had not been brought into play for years, were seen to wipe suspicious moisture from their eyes.*[58]

Bob Fitzsimmons came from a culture wherein fair play was highly honored, which made him painfully aware of the physical inequalities between himself and the man he had deprived of the middleweight title.

For this reason, he took a pass on accepting the *National Police Gazette* Diamond Belt.

Reporters sought out the pugilistic guru John L. Sullivan for his opinion. When asked how he accounted for Dempsey's defeat, his reply was classic John L.:

> *"How do I account for it? You might as well ask me to account for the spots of the sun. It is one of those things that can't be accounted for. Well I guess it's all up with Dempsey now."*
>
> *And the big fellow heaved a four-horse power sigh. "He'll never recover from this licking. The poor fellow's heart must be broken. I'm going to turn in. Good-night."*[59]

The following day, the newspapers released a statement by Dempsey that it was time to retire. He emphatically stated that he would not engage in another fight. He further reminded the gathering of reporters of his nuptial promise and that it was his wife's expressed wishes that he settle in Portland, Oregon. He planned to take up the traditional occupation of ex-prizefighters and open a saloon. Those who knew him best suspected that he was speaking from the pain of humiliation following defeat—a condition unfamiliar to him. They knew he would be back in the ring he loved once he got used to the suffering of being a has-been.

# 9

# The Pastime at the Cyclorama

After his defeat in New Orleans, Dempsey found that many members of the press are not kind to losers, no matter how often they had won before, but the sporting world still honored its heroes. A benefit in his honor was held at the Pacific Athletic Club in San Francisco, with a panel of popular doctors of the fistic science that included Young Mitchell. It was a tradition, of sorts, for losing prizefighters to hold benefit sparring matches to defray the money lost. Dempsey had done as much for Dave Campbell, passing the hat on the steamboat years before. Fitzsimmons had offered to hold one in New Orleans for his opponent, but Dempsey refused, saying it would look bad for him.

## HOMECOMING?

On All Hallows Eve 1891, Jack and his family arrived in Astoria en route to Portland from San Francisco aboard the steamship *Columbia*. When they had left Portland, Dempsey was fast approaching bankruptcy, but now he had some $3,800 in his vest pocket from the event at the Pacific Club. (In talking with a reporter, the treasurer of the event embellished an extra zero, telling him it was $38,000,[60] a well-intentioned act that did Dempsey no good.) This summary of the affair was published in several Oregon newspapers:

A rare glimpse of the Cyclorama Building where the Pastime Club began. Detail from a panorama. *Author's collection.*

> *The dazzling success of genial Jack is enough to make a minister who labors 38 years to make that amount of money feel as though the man who fights the devil hasn't quite as good a thing as the man who fights his fellow man.*[61]

There was no parade with brass band and banners to meet Dempsey when he finally came into Portland to stay. Not only did he abhor publicity, but he also had been in and out of Portland many times since his marriage to a Portland girl. In addition, he was a bit of a pugilistic gadfly, popping off on boats and trains at the arrival of a telegram or the drop of a towel. It was a fact that Portland sportsmen thought of him as one of their own, even though Brooklyn, New York, had never relinquished its claim on the great Nonpareil. He had purchased (and later mortgaged and then forfeited) a house for his family in East Portland, near where Maggie's parents and brother lived.

By the time Jack Dempsey kept his wedding promise, eight years had passed, East Portland had dropped the uppercase *E* from its name (having been incorporated into the coming metropolis) and a new skyline was rising across the Willamette. Rusty old mansions and sagging, wood-framed commercial buildings in the city's core were being pulled down and replaced with reassuring edifices built of good brick, stone and concrete.

## DEMPSEY IS ILL

Ex-champion Dempsey and his new sparring partner, Young Mitchell, were on the move within a few weeks, having signed with the Harry Williams Variety Company of New York to appear in a touring show. It was Dempsey's intention to turn Young Mitchell into a prizefighter of the first order as they trained and sparred together. This plan would have been an easy way for Dempsey to make some money and keep his name in the lights had it worked. Dempsey and Mitchell, accompanied by their wives, arrived in Jersey City aboard the Pennsylvania Limited on Saturday, November 14, 1891. The following Tuesday, Dempsey was taken suddenly, frighteningly ill, making it impossible to fulfill his engagement at the Hyde and Behman's Theater in Brooklyn—an event that he would never have missed could he have helped it.

The ex-champion was gaunt and feverish and took to his bed in the hotel, attended by his wife and friends. The doctors who examined him no doubt knew that it was tuberculosis—"incipient consumption" was the phrase they would have used to describe it had they been in the habit of being honest with their patients. It was so obvious that the eager newsmen soon got hold of it, either from Dempsey's doctors or from some other source, spreading it across the nation's newswires. The report included the ominous words "the beginning of the end for Dempsey." All this media attention made the Nonpareil more determined than ever to get over his "bilious fever" (his doctor's words) and back into the ring. It may be that the world doesn't love a loser, but few people, indeed, will bother to visit a sick man. In spite of his desire to get out of bed and back to slogging in the ring, the illness cut short his theater tour and brought him, at last, along with his wife and daughters, to Portland. If this illness were to turn out to be "incipient consumption," then exertion and running around the countryside was the worst possible plan of action.

## PROFESSOR DEMPSEY THE NONPAREIL SETTLES DOWN

A few weeks later, beneath the headline "Professor Dempsey—the Nonpareil Settles Down," the *Oregonian*[62] announced Jack Dempsey's appointment as general manager of the Pastime Club. The club was the joint effort of Dempsey and some wealthy backers (who assumed Jack, too, was wealthy) attempting to give Portland a first-class venue for the fistic science, like the clubs in New York, Chicago, New Orleans and San Francisco. This idea delighted many Portlanders, like the working-class Irish of Slabtown or any number of sportsmen. The same idea struck fear and indignation into the hearts of many others—say, the wealthy hill dwellers, the manifold suffragettes and the parsons in their black preaching jackets (like my grandfather). This would have made Maggie and the rest of the Brady family, one assumes, quite happy. "A regular job, no more fighting, no more blood, Jack will turn out to be a peach! Wait and see!" some family members may have thought. He was now manager of a club, albeit one without a clubhouse or venue.

## THE GREAT GETTYSBURG CYCLORAMA OF PORTLAND

During the absence of the Dempsey family, one of the many changes to downtown Portland was the block between Third and Fourth and Ash and Pine Streets housing the mansion built by the pioneer sea captain and entrepreneur R.R. Thompson. The mansion had been carefully lifted from its prominent place mid-block and moved to the edge of the property to make a viable space for a commercial building. The mansion then became, like so many of its disgraced brethren, divided into apartments.

In the fall of 1887, the spot in the middle of the block vacated by the mansion was leased for an initial nine years by the Portland Cyclorama Company. This company constructed in this space a large brick building of circular design to house its exhibits—the foremost being the Battle of Gettysburg. The exhibit had a dramatic entrance leading to a winding, underground passage to the middle of the building. The visitors then walked into the exhibit in its very center, being met with an enormous 360-degree painting of the raging battle, complete with sound effects and the smell of gunpowder. In late Victorian days, this was among the greatest multimedia events imaginable. The Cyclorama opened to the public on December 30, 1887, with throngs of people arriving from all over Oregon and southern Washington Territory. During this era, Cycloramas were being constructed as tourist attractions in cities around the country, with the favorite subject being the Battle of Gettysburg, so it wasn't long before the novelty wore off. In Portland, the exhibit lasted only a few years before the investors in the company were scrambling to come up with the lease money.

When Jack Dempsey turned his eye toward settling in Portland, he knew that the only way he could make a go of it here was if Portland had an athletic club to match the great prizefighting venues in larger cities. Prizefighting was a legal gray area whose hues grew brighter or darker depending on the whims of society. The "swells" from Nob Hill and Portland Heights could box at the Multnomah Club under the careful eye of a boxing "professor," but let someone from Goose Hollow, Slabtown or East Portland start punching away on someone in a sporting saloon and a lookout had to be kept for the police. If Portland were to become a major prizefighting city, it would need to have a sporting club of which to be proud—or so Dempsey's thoughts must have run when he began making immediate arrangements with two other investors to lease the empty Cyclorama Building.

The Pastime Club had been collecting subscribers and running glove matches in anticipation of a clubhouse and had reported four hundred members whose initiation fees were $5.00, with yearly membership at $2.50. As ideals went, the old Cyclorama Building was an ideal venue. The plans for remodeling, estimated to cost $5,000.00, included a balcony seating two thousand spectators and a main floor with seating for three thousand. They would no longer use the winding, subterranean entrance but sensible, street-level doors. In addition, the venue would house a café dispensing food and booze to those attending the matches. Optimism among Portland sportsmen was high, as was opposition. It was believed by most nonsportsmen that where there were fisticuffs, there was crime, drunkenness, cussing, tobacco use and many other things society could well do without. These folks would just as soon see a large, brick French bordello open in downtown as to see the Cyclorama turned into a boxing club. Of course, at that time in Portland, there was no shortage of bordellos, bagnios, whorehouses or cribs—French or otherwise—where a variety of pimps could ply their trade.

The club went into business on March 22, 1892, even before all the painted panels of the Gettysburg exhibit were taken away and with the ring yet to be moved to its central location. The opening event was between Tommy West of Portland and Charles Hall of Chicago, with the main attraction being a fight between middleweights Charles Gleason and Ed Burke, with Jack Dempsey as referee. The *San Francisco Call* reported the event, mentioning that "[the Pastime Club] has one of the finest clubrooms in America. It is situated in the Cyclorama building, and is 103 feet in diameter. It will seat 5,000 people."[63]

Over the next several months, it seemed as though the club were settling into a comfortable position in the Portland sporting world. The lineup of talent was impressive for 1892, with matches between such fistic luminaries as George Lavigne versus Harry Jones, Pasty Cardiff versus Billy Kough, Charley Gleason versus Ed Burke and Paddy Smith versus Charles Bogan, and (for the information of Portland history buffs) it also included the introduction of a spry young scrapper whom the papers referred to as "Billy Smith of Boston." On the evening of May 26, Billy Smith took on Tommy West[64] in a little remarked upon event of which boxing historians should take note. The match was concluded to be a draw by referee Jack Dempsey.

The clubhouse, with a private telegraph setup, also served as a safe place to bet on matches taking place elsewhere. It was Dempsey's expressed purpose that the shenanigans that caused false results to be exhibited on bulletin boards in saloons and cigar stores would not be permitted. The venue, larger even than the Mechanic's Pavilion, was a building with civic importance, so Dempsey made every attempt to make it available for public service, such as political meetings, local charity works, fire department dances and such. It was one small effort to quell the growing tide of opposition to his sport.

## INSOLVENT?

Of several dark clouds gathering over Dempsey's head that year, what seemed most immediate was his difficulty in feeding his investors real, honest-to-God greenbacks. With Dempsey, greenbacks had a habit of growing wings. The newspapers had earlier printed an article accusing him of squandering a fortune, which regrettably was true. His way of "squandering," as those close to him knew, was that he had too many "friends" in need. As he came from proud, working poverty, it is certain he knew plenty of folks with genuine, life-

The Exposition Building (later a skating rink) at Eighteenth and Burnside. *Sketched by author from a damaged photograph.*

threatening needs. Having been a young fool myself, I can appreciate that Dempsey—who thought himself invincible (within certain weight limits)—must have thought that his "cash machine" of a career was limitless. Nevertheless, when the investors came a-knocking, Dempsey's piggy bank was empty. The two other investors—a rich sporting man named R.S. Smith and Pat Powers, a local "Tammany boss" and owner of racehorses—took Dempsey to court in early July 1892, saying that he had led them to believe he was rolling in clover when he was actually insolvent. Dempsey's response was, for him, typical: "I am not insolvent! I may not have money, but I can get money."

## TOO HONEST? BAD MANAGER?

The newspaper reports on this lawsuit are almost comical, as the same report is spun according to the newspaper editor's bias toward "glove contests." The *Seattle Post-Intelligencer* reported the news beneath a headline that read: "JACK DEMPSEY A BAD MANAGER. His Prize-Fight Club Broken Up and He Himself Sued for an Accounting."

The *Los Angeles Herald* put the same information into an article whose headline read: "HONEST DEMPSEY: He Allows the Portland Pastime Club to

Be Wound Up." The article included information supplied by Dempsey's friends that the saintly Jack Dempsey had partners who wanted him to throw fights in their favor. When he refused to do so, they came down on him in court. This story is more suited to hagiography than to news reporting. It is far more believable that Jack Dempsey's business management skills were nowhere close to his boxing instruction skills and that the business end suffered beneath his delusion that his skills were a limitless source of cash. Both takes on the story were incorrect. The Pastime Club was allowed to continue on in the Cyclorama Building for the time being, but the clock was now ticking rather loudly that time was running out.

## BILLY MABER VERSUS BILLY SMITH

On the last night of summer 1892, the Australian ruffian Billy Maber was pitted against the wild and unpredictable youth Billy Smith in the Pastime Club—still in the old Cyclorama. To witness this contest were 1,500 paying spectators and Chief Spencer, who sat in the press box wearing a stoic expression as though he were Julius Caesar deciding the fate of a gladiator. The crowd was aware of the importance of the presence of the police chief, as reports were circling that the district attorney was fed up with the "farce" of glove contests.

The *Oregonian* report of the match was ripe with irony, saying that the event was environed with "a deep fringe of oratory," which meant that Jack Dempsey was bending over backward to try to convince the chief of police that it was a scientific exhibition and not a sockfest. He is quoted as saying:

> *This will be a scientific set-to, and nothing else. If at anytime I become convinced that one of the men cannot possibly win the contest, I shall award it to his opponent. The days of prize-fights and prize-ring brutality are over. This will be a scientific contest.*[65]

The crowd applauded this with hoots and whistles of approval. The bout proceeded through twenty-three punishing rounds in which the "Australian" was often cowed by the "Bostonian's" vicious whirlwind of pummeling. In the end, the match and the $1,000 prize were Billy Smith's. As a sort of entertaining catharsis, Billy Maber got up on a chair in the middle of the ring and apologized to the crowd for being whipped: "I don't know what was the

A very young Billy Smith, an early cabinet card. *Author's collection.*

matter with me tonight, but I didn't feel right, and my legs gave out, and I was not feeling right."

This also brought hoots and whistles of approval. Who could possibly deem that such an event was a "prizefight" when the loser was able to stand up on a chair and shout out an apology? It seems that District Attorney Hume was willing to deem such an event a prizefight. The fight had been on a Tuesday night; by Friday, a grand jury had also deemed such an event a prizefight, issuing warrants for the likes of Billy Maber, Billy Smith, Jack Dempsey, old Joe Taylor, Gus Herget and Billy Hennesey requiring $1,500 bonds. Dempsey was released immediately, whereupon he went to a cigar store and returned with tobacco and cigars in case he would have difficulty in securing bonds for his friends. Eventually, bondsmen were found.

When the trial took place in November, the first ones in the dock were the fighters themselves. The main witnesses for the prosecution were police officers Sheriff Kelly and Chief Deputy Sheriff Marquam (neither the chief of police nor the police captain could attend the trial). These officers testified that the contest was not brutal and was indeed somewhat "scientific." Since most of the testimony agreed on these issues, the jury was out for less than ten minutes before arriving at a not guilty verdict. Then the district attorney dropped the cases against Dempsey and the other defendants, and the fight against "glove contests" was knocked off course for the time being.

Dempsey's intention to settle down in Portland was real, but he was driven back into the ring by two strong forces: his own self-esteem and his empty bank account. Everything sucked money and energy from him, not the least being the Pastime Club itself. The only logical (in his mind) way forward was for him to go headlong (to borrow a phrase from William Shakespeare) "once more unto the breach, dear friends, once more,"[66]—which, for his health's sake, was the wrong move completely. His mission was clear: make more money to bail himself and the club out of debt.

Dempsey's personal physician was the well-known and well-loved (by "progressives") Dr. Harry Lane.[67] He did not see fit to tell Jack that he was dying of tuberculosis, thinking that the news would hasten his demise. Neither did Dr. Lane, at that time, see fit to tell Dempsey's wife (this being the standard practice of physicians at the time). Dempsey, having no clue about the reality of his condition, turned over the management of the Pastime Club to a couple of good friends: Jack Grant from Astoria and Jack Day, a Portland pugilist and referee. Grant also was recognized as an excellent referee, and he had interesting political connections, being the brother, and sometimes partner, of Peter Grant, one of the owners of the Portland Club casino and the city's largest sailor's boardinghouse.

## FAREWELL BENEFIT FIZZLES

Dempsey had to convince not only himself and his family but also the entire world that he was not finished as a fighter. To illustrate this, a retrospective on the sport published in the *Los Angeles Herald* in February contained what was practically a eulogy of the ex-champion that ended with the words: "There is lots of good material in that little fellow, even though his days as a fighting man are well passed away."[68]

At the end of March, Gus Tuthill, Dempsey's old backer, posted a challenge to the effect that he would back Dempsey, "having regained his health,"

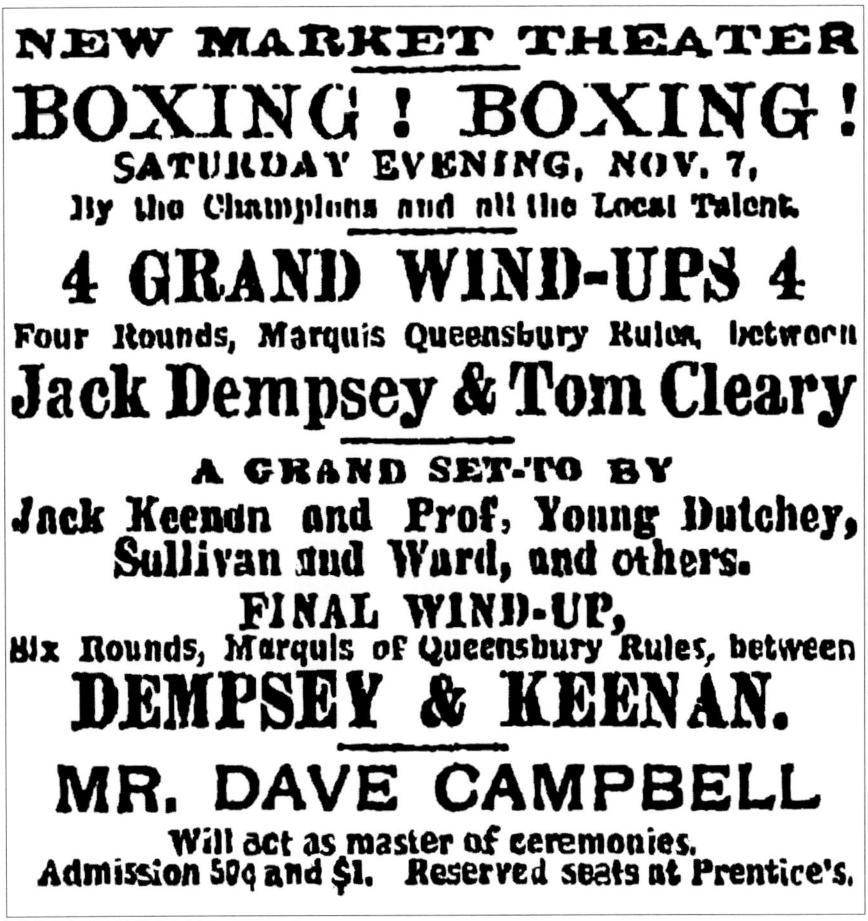


Dempsey-Cleary match. *Facsimile of an advertisement in the* Morning Oregonian, *November 6, 1885.*

to the sum of $2,500 against any man alive under 140 pounds. By April, Dempsey had made arrangements to go east to begin accepting some of the many challenges coming at him. Even though he had lost his title, he was still viewed as the unbeatable Nonpareil; in other words, fair game. It may be that word that he was weakening was circulating, encouraging opponents who were willing to take any advantage to further their career. Whether this was a sign of waning support, I can't say, but Dempsey was promised by a whole slew of gladiators that they would participate in his April benefit to raise money for his trip east. The event was dismal. Only about two hundred spectators and almost none of the promised talent showed. Dempsey offered everyone their money back and free entertainment, but few, if any, took him up on a refund. He then threw together an ad hoc event for the people on hand and demonstrated his own pugilistic talents. It was a lame sort of farewell, but then Portland was not as crazy about Dempsey as a Brooklyn, New Yorker, as it had been of Dempsey the new Portland boy.

On the evening of May 8, without fanfare, the Dempsey family left by train for New York, leaving behind a mess of legal troubles for others to sort out. It was understood at the time that he would fight "Mysterious" Billy Smith before the Coney Island Athletic Club in June for a purse of $6,000. Jack had not fought professionally since being knocked out by Fitzsimmons, yet he had been the recipient of numerous challenges, complete with financial incentives and large purses. It is almost inconceivable that a man with advancing tuberculosis would be unaware of a weakening of his lungs and body. However, Dempsey always maintained that he was in the best of health; that is, until his final weeks on this earth.

## BACK INTO THE BREACH

On May 3, the news went out on the wires that Jack Dempsey and "Mysterious" Billy Smith were matched to fight at the Coney Island Club on June 30 for a purse of $6,000 and the welterweight championship of the world. A week later, while staying at the Anderson House, a small hotel in Lynn, Massachusetts, Minnie Smith, the eighteen-year-old new bride of Billy Smith, suddenly died of food poisoning. Under the circumstances, the Coney Island Club officers felt compelled to allow Billy Smith out of his contract so that he could accompany his wife's body by train back to his adopted home in Portland, Oregon, where she was to be buried. Billy was just shy of his twenty-second birthday when his wife died. The match was delayed, being reset for July 24 at the Coney Island Club.

Halfway through the month of June, the sporting men of the Coney Island Club noticed that the Nonpareil was not to be found and none of the normal sources close to the ex-champion seemed to have any inkling of where he was secluding himself. He had, as yet, not shown up to sign the new articles to fight Billy Smith. Some of the gentlemen of the club had one thousand postal cards sent to athletic resorts around the country with the following message:

> *Lost, strayed or stolen—one middle-weight pugilist, of blond complexion, with mild blue eyes. Answers to the name Jack Dempsey. Any information regarding the above cheerfully received by the Coney Island Athletic Club.*[69]

After several days, it became apparent that the Dempsey family had taken a powder back to Oregon, and there was no mystery or disappearance. The nervousness of his peers does show, however, a great deal of anxiety about Jack Dempsey as a rock solid investment. Then, several weeks later, the Coney Island Club announced the meet was off for the time being. The report declared that in the absence of the fighters, it was impossible for the board of directors to have "tangible proof" that the men were in condition for the match. This was a thinly veiled dig. Surely there would be no reason for assuming that Billy Smith was unfit, but Dempsey was a different story.

It was a match that seemed to be postponed until doomsday. There was another contender, an English pugilist named Dick Burge, who had made his way to America after being challenged by Dempsey through the office of Richard K. Fox. After arriving in New York, it became apparent that the Coney Island Club was not going to offer a purse for the battle, and if the Coney Island Club, where Dempsey was bound to draw big, was out, then no other club would touch the fight. In the end, Burge had to return back across the Atlantic disappointed at having not met with the Nonpareil.

## INSANE?

To help put an end to the flood of rumors that Jack Dempsey was a "galloping consumptive," in October of that year, both Billy Delaney and James J. Corbett wrote open letters, published by the wire press, declaring their eyewitness accounts of Jack Dempsey's full recovery from his former illness and testifying of his current robust health. Then, in November, the news was published abroad that Jack Dempsey was going to go back on the New York stage with a sparring part in a William Brady Company comedy called *The Bottom of the Sea*.[70] A few days after this news went to press, the following announcement appeared, inexplicable in its brevity: "Jack Dempsey, the once champion middle-weight pugilist, has been confined in a private insane asylum at Chicago, and his match with Dick Burge, the English champion, is off."[71]

Then, two days later, New York papers announced Dempsey's arrival and willingness to fight the Englishman in question. On November 14, the day following his arrival in New York, the *Evening World* reported the success of *The Bottom of the Sea* at the H.R. Jacob's Theater, with an exciting sparring session by Jack Dempsey and Denny Costigan.

Where the report of the Chicago insane asylum came from is a mystery. At his arrival in New York, Dempsey's health seemed fine. It is a common trait of tuberculosis that sufferers will go through a period of feeling good, only to have the disease return stronger and more vicious than before. It is also not at all unusual for sufferers to assume that they are cured, resuming vigorous activity that can serve only to bring a hasty relapse.

For someone ruled insane or at the end of his rope, Dempsey was seen to be quite active, sparring in the William Brady play through most of January 1894 and then traveling to Jacksonville, Florida, with James J. Corbett to second him in his successful match against another Englishman, Charles Mitchell. The match was to be fought at the Duval Athletic Club for $5,000 and the heavyweight championship. Throughout the weeks surrounding that world-famous match, Dempsey's name was reassuringly mentioned among the pugilists. The nation's newswires also repeated the story of how Dempsey, as Corbett's second, was responsible to check the soundness and safety of the ring. He found, upon examination, that the stage was unstable beneath his feet and the rope posts were bare metal when the contract called for padding. When the management of the Duval Athletic Club was obstinate, refusing to make the required changes, Dempsey began to use the sort of language that he famously "only used in the absence of women." In one report, this is amusingly described as "much profane simile." With words he was certain his southern hosts would understand, he assured the club management that Corbett would not fight unless the corrections were made. Once the message got across, management got busy and fixed the problems post haste or, as one report put it, "with such motion as is the antebellum interpretation of

The Coney Island Clubhouse being set up for the motion picture filming. *From American Mutoscope & Biograph Co., 1899, Library of Congress LC-USZ62-102696.*

'haste.'" The fight went on, and in the end, "Gentleman" Jim Corbett's title was declared safe and he became a wealthier man.

As the year 1894 moved on into summer, it began to be apparent that Jack Dempsey, who had fought only one minor prizefight since his defeat by Fitzsimmons, had managed, of recent days, to have every prospective bout turn into a mirage. Whether this was thought to be by accident or design depended on the level of cynicism or charity in the eye of the beholder. However, Dempsey fans, always hungry for a good story, were fed a yarn by Denny Costigan. The yarn was picked up by the wires and became a small diversion to newspaper readers at breakfast counters and on trolley cars across the great American continent now joined, at the speed of electricity, by telegraph wires.

It seems Denny Costigan met some ladies who were impressed that he was a fighter who sparred with the great Nonpareil. Costigan then invited the ladies to enjoy a box seat and promised them that they would see him give the great Jack Dempsey a run for his money. Dempsey noticed right off the bat that his partner was more than a little animated. He was whispering to him to "go easy" when he began to notice the glances Costigan was throwing to a certain box seat full of young ladies. When it became clear to Dempsey what Costigan was up to, he set about chasing Costigan around the stage, batting his ears at every opportunity. At the end of this embarrassing display, Dempsey whispered to his partner, "Say, Costigan, always consult me when you want to make a star play. I deserve your confidence."[72] It was another good lesson from the forthright Irishman, and in some ways it made better press than a knockout blow.

By the end of summer, Dempsey had arranged another prizefight with another Australian, Billy McCarthy, to be fought before the Auditorium Athletic Club of New Orleans in early September. The bout was fairly unremarkable. It became twenty rounds of tit for tat, with McCarthy dancing out of reach, or clinching, and Dempsey unable to "put him to sleep." At the end, it was declared a draw, and the prize money was divided.

Then, a chance for Dempsey to obtain another title came into view in the person of one Tommy Ryan. It was an opportunity to earn a $5,000 prize and the welterweight championship of the world. When Dempsey arrived in New Orleans in December, it was reported that he was in excellent condition. In fact, the word on the newswires went under the headline "DEMPSEY IN FINE SHAPE" with the article out of New Orleans reading, in part: "Dempsey's stock will probably improve now that investors have an opportunity of seeing him and judging for themselves as to his condition."[73]

At the very last minute, a monkey wrench hit the gears in motion for the match. The night before the Dempsey/Ryan bout, "Kid" Lavigne was pitted against the New Orleans favorite, a local boy named Andy Bowen, lightweight champion of the South. At the end on the eighteenth round, Bowen was knocked out, falling and smashing his head on the floor, which should have been padded. The fall killed him, bringing arrests to all involved and an end to prizefighting in New Orleans for the time being. Later, it was shown by the coroner's report that the unpadded floor had more to do with the death than the knockout blow. This exonerated Lavigne and got prizefighting back on the rails in New Orleans. The Jack Dempsey/Tommy Ryan affair was rescheduled for mid-January, to take place at the Seaside Athletic Club on Coney Island.

This report of Dempsey's robust health was in mid-December. Things had changed by January 5, when the night edition of New York's *Evening World* ran a report stating that once again Jack Dempsey was "lost, stolen, or strayed" and that his friends and supporters knew not where to find him. The article went on to remind readers how the Nonpareil had disappeared in a puff of smoke prior to the match with Billy Smith. The insult to the injury of these words was that it was coming from a New York paper normally sympathetic to hometown boys. About this time, reports began to surface that Jack was "moody," or that he missed his family in Portland or that he had been drinking, but the fact remained: he had disappeared from New Orleans and had not yet returned to New York to start training for a match that was just around the corner.

On January 10, Dempsey arrived in Gotham from New Orleans aboard the steamer *Hudson*. He had left New Orleans unnoticed and arrived unannounced, and he was met by only one friend at the pier. His friend, Jack Kennedy, a pal from his Brooklyn days, told the press that he was "looking heavy and strong."

On January 15, Tommy Ryan arrived from Chicago with pugilist Joe Choyinski. He looked like a bundle of compressed energy in the best of health. The next day it was reported that, upon observation of his workout at the Manhattan Athletic Club, he was the "cleverest bag puncher and rope jumper the world has ever seen."

On January 18, the night of the battle, the night edition of the *Evening World* stated flatly:

> *Although little has been said of Dempsey's condition, it cannot be disguised that he is not in the best of shape. This information has not been given out to the public, but it is known by "The Evening World" that Jack has been under medical advice for throat and chest trouble during the past week, and that on Wednesday he was drinking whiskey, as he said, by order of Dr. Ward, his attending physician. Whiskey has been proven poor stuff to train on, as "The Evening World" pointed out on a previous occasion.*

The next issue of the *Evening World* told of a whole world of hurt coming Jack Dempsey's way. In a series of headlines, line upon line, the terrible truth became known:

> *DEMPSEY'S SHADOW.*
> *A Ghost of the "Nonpareil" Faced Ryan Last Night.*
> *One Blow Might Have Killed Him, but Tommy Was Generous.*
> *Shouts of Applause Quickly Turn to Jibes for the Ex-Champion.*[74]

The *Evening World* was eloquent in its self-aggrandizing congratulations for predicting the outcome, as well as scathing in its denunciations of Dempsey as a deluded drunken has-been who wasted a lot of other people's time and money. The paper also had little use for the cadre of friends who insulated the ex-champion from scrutiny and gave glowing reports of his good health to news reporters. It was a horrible fall due to a number of issues unnamed at the time. The word "consumption" isn't used (the word "tuberculosis" was not in common use at the time). The paper assumed that Dempsey's trouble was due to laziness and drunkenness.

The fight itself was a farce from the start. As Dempsey entered the ring, his four thousand or so admirers "screamed themselves hoarse at his appearing." When his cloak fell away from him, the report continued, he stood there "a sorry spectacle of tottering weakness." Ryan could see that one good punch would end the farce, but it could also end the ex-champion's days on earth, so the Chicago boy danced around the reeling specter as a kid around an arthritic grandfather, hoping to wear him out. After a short minute of this, the crowd turned and began to shout, "Take him off!" and "Dempsey's drunk!" while many disgusted spectators began to fill the aisles to leave, not wishing to view the unsightly fall of their former hero.

The farce continued into the third lame round, with Tommy Ryan gently holding Dempsey with one hand while tapping him with the other in an attempt to make him stop, short of killing him. Finally, mercifully, the referee called an end to the affair, and Dempsey was shuffled off to a Brooklyn hideout.

The *Evening World*'s report of the affair, though ungracious, was factual, mentioning even the "black bottle" that Dempsey's seconds had ready for him containing "his enemy," presumably the whiskey the quack Ward had prescribed along with a phony-baloney diagnosis of "throat and lung trouble." Upon entering the dressing rooms of the arena, it was obvious Dempsey was drunk. Tommy Ryan's manager, the esteemed "Parson" Davies, the man who at that time had put black pugilist Peter Jackson in a national tour of *Uncle Tom's Cabin*, tried to influence Dempsey before the match after watching and detecting an undisguisable cloud of whiskey fumes. His straight talk probably went something like this: "Look here, Dempsey. You are drunk and disgusting! Forfeit the match now and save your honor. If the people see you like this, you will be ruined and despised for the sot that you are!" Dempsey was, by this time, at the stage of belligerence well known to anyone who has had dealings with alcohol addiction; reasoning with him was out of the question. Dempsey had never been known to have a problem with the bottle, but now, thanks to Davies, it was assumed that he was just another of the many Irishmen to fall victim to the demons of booze.

The fall from pugilistic greatness was one thing and could be taken in stride by most men; the fall of one's honor as a man of dignity and clear-eyed sobriety was another sort of fall entirely. The only men who knew the truth were the medical men with the skills to diagnose tuberculosis from visible clues. Dempsey was far from where he belonged, far from the kind help of his loving family, the kindly care of good old Dr. Harry Lane and the laughter of his lovely daughters. The tuberculosis had come back, as it does, with a vengeance, and he would not live out the year.

It may be that had he met Ryan in New Orleans, as originally planned, he would have been fit enough to make a stand. But if this kind of speculation was of any value, Andy Bowen, whose death had caused the delay of the fight, would still be walking up and down Bourbon Street with his *petite amie* instead of moldering in a cement sarcophagus in the Saint Louis Cemetery on Basin Street.

# 10

# Portland's Mysterioso

## L.H. Gregory Listens to Billy's Mysterious Baloney

Six years before his death in 1937, an arthritic old pugilist who was once called "Billy Smith of Boston" and later "Mysterious" Billy Smith recounted some of his old yarns to sportswriter L.H. Gregory of the *Oregonian*. He repeated his well-worn fiction about being born in Maine,[75] to which he added a further fiction that he was the son of a sea captain.

According to Gregory, "Billy could talk 'clews' and 'braces' and 'sailing close-hauled' and such, with any old sailor, but he didn't like the life." Smith related to Gregory how he had been handy with his fists since he was a lad and how, had his father known of his aspirations to be a prizefighter, he would have sent him to sea in a whaling ship—a standard treatment for the wayward sons of mariners. At first, he was managed by his brother. He went to Boston and fought under an assumed name so his father would not hear of it. After winning a string of victories, he appeared on the West Coast using the name by which he was normally called: "Billy Smith." Because the Australian Billy Smith was whacking people out of the ring around San Francisco, he became "Billy Smith of Boston." Seeing reports of these bouts caused a writer for the *Boston Police News* to wonder (having never heard of him in Boston), "Who is this mysterious Billy Smith?" Thus was created the moniker, famous to the ages, "Mysterious" Billy Smith (caveat: this is

"Mysterious" Billy Smith in Portland in 1892, driving a sully. *Press photo, courtesy of Oregon Historical Society, 009058.*

the account given to Gregory by Mr. Smith himself, a man not know for his great concern with historical accuracy).

Before Smith was enthralled by the charm of old Portland, he had already made a small name for himself. He started his career in 1891, but as fate (or something) would have it, Billy Smith the Australian was making a name for himself as well. A casual glance at dozens of news clippings tells me that Billy wasn't completely "Mysterious" Billy Smith until 1905. It is also apparent that Smith needed to keep his origins secret. Americans were, in those days, far more xenophobic and chauvinistic than in later years. It was important to Smith that he be an American native, and with a name like "Smith" at a time when birth records were not kept as vigorously as they are today, it was possible for him to shift his birthplace by a few dozen miles, including across an international border.

Smith had this mystery, but his public persona was that of a two-dimensional, two-bit hood with an uncanny knack for knowing when the referee wasn't looking. In the superstitious world of pugilism, a little mystery added kick to his punch, making him (to steal words from Terry Malloy)[76] a "real contender." Smith had what we hacks often call a "varied and colorful career." His efforts in the world of "shipping sailors" (known also as "shanghaiing") I have mentioned in some detail in my other books, this being an attempt at a profession that brought Smith more headache than reward. His skill at pony racing was well known in his day, as was that of buying and selling good racehorses. Finally, after Prohibition, he was a local Albina neighborhood character and dispenser of suds in his cozy beer tavern, Champion's Rest.

His career as a prizefighter, though, was one of a bright, rising star, noticed by the world at its gleaming zenith—then, as the star floated slowly downward, the gradient of its luminance lessened into darkness. Then it was gone, albeit the fall lasted for years. Like Jack Dempsey, Billy Smith started his career fighting bare-fisted under London rules at a time when the rules changed back and forth with the wind. Also like Dempsey, Smith didn't have to knock too many people's brains out to get noticed.

When he first came to Portland, it was early in his career, just prior to his title match. He arrived on April 9, 1892, aboard a steamship from San Francisco in the company of "Kid" Lavigne.[77] Lavigne was in town to hammer out a deal with Dempsey. Smith, on the other hand, was a fighter without a fight—albeit a good fighter, for which Lavigne could vouch. Smith had yet to win any coveted crown. Lavigne, on the other hand, could say that he was the "featherweight champion of Michigan." Besides, Lavigne was the "Saginaw Kid." Billy Smith was just plain Billy Smith.

In the six months Smith spent in Portland, he fought three good prizefights at the Pastime Club: two wins and one draw. The last match was with Billy "Shadow" Maber, fresh off the boat from Australia. It was the match that landed the fighters and everyone else involved in jail on the charge of prizefighting.

## WIGWAM AND CONEY ISLAND BOUTS

After leaving Portland, Billy Smith's career took off. His next bout was at the Wigwam Theater in San Francisco in December 1892, when in fourteen rounds he won a match against Danny Needham (aka the "Saint Paul Terror") that gave him access to the title of welterweight champion. It was a title he needed to defend that April at the Coney Island Athletic Club against the Australian Tom Williams. The match was for a $5,000 purse and the welterweight championship of the world. The odds were seen to be in the Australian's favor, and so went the betting of the New York gamblers. The match didn't even garner a lot of interest for a title match.

On April 17, 1893, the evening of the match, "Billy Smith of Boston" was in his corner with a few friends from San Francisco, a tiny island of Billy Smith fans in a sea of opposition. The first round, the two lay aside the usual formalities and fell on each other like angry roosters, knocking each other down in flurries of hard punches.

By the beginning of round two, the spectators were all alert to the fact that an unusually fierce battle was unfolding before their eyes. The two went at it again, but each one had lost a bit of vigor; in fact, Williams had lost so much steam that by the end of the round he was unable to rise, completely exhausted. Billy Smith of Boston was off to a great start, with $5,000 in his pocket and a championship. As the greater portion of the New York audience had wagered against Smith, his name was mud in Gotham. However, puzzled fans of pugilistic science in Boston were made proud by the mysterious stranger.

## THE MYSTERIOUS STRANGER RETURNS

During the time Smith had been away from Portland, he was involved in no fewer than seventy-five professional prizefights—for the most part, either winning or drawing, although his losses were starting to add up. He had won the middleweight championship in August 1898, fighting Matty Mathews at the Lenox Athletic Club in New York, and then lost it to Rube Ferns on one of his famous fouls in January 1900. He had been living out of a suitcase for years, although he had planned to settle in Portland with his wife, Minnie, before her sudden death while on the road with Smith. Since Boston was no real home, Portland must have seemed a very good prospect, especially considering the condition of Billy Smith when he arrived by train from California that quiet Tuesday evening, August 27, 1901. Rooms had been prepared for Smith at the Mikado Hotel at 101 Sixth Street (old address system), a favorite with traveling fighters. The hotel had a gym that was set up for sparring practice and could be used exclusively by the fighters and their partners. The Pastime Club had booked him for a match against yet another "antipodean pugilist," Tom Tracy. However, when Tracy arrived, he was too sick to fight, and the match was postponed until October.

Dempsey's old Pastime Club was still going strong under the direction of the two Jacks, Grant and Day, but now the club used rooms at the Exposition Building, lacking a clubhouse of its own. Shortly after July 4, 1893, the club lost the lease on the old Cyclorama Building to a Pacific Coast theater manager named John Cort. Cort spent a fortune remodeling the building as the Alhambra Theater, to be a venue for musical comedy of the English music hall tradition.[78] This may have worked in Victoria, British Columbia, but it was a surefire shot to the foot in Portland, where tastes ran more to the slapstick side of the comic masque and the *slam-bang!* sport of fists.

The long-awaited match took place on October 26, 1901, at the Pastime Club rooms at the Exhibition Building. The event was written up as a "hugging match" lasting twenty tedious rounds. The match consisted largely of both Smith and Tracy "grunting, hugging, and feinting" like a couple of adolescent brown bears romping at City Park Zoo. When it was finally over, the referee called it a draw. This surprised no one; in fact, the *Oregonian* reported, "According to agreement Referee Acton called it a draw." The fact was: Billy Smith had not won a fight since September 1900 in a bout against Young Jackson. He would not be able to live on draws and split winnings forever.

## FOUL FIGHTING AND DIRTY TRICKS

Realizing that he had to redeem himself in the eyes of the Portland public, Smith agreed to a match with Al Neil, welterweight champion from California. The match was set for November 18, 1901, at the clubrooms in the Exposition Building. To train for this bout, Smith would run out Macadam to the White House, where he would hit the handball court. Then he would spend his afternoons back at the Mikado punching bags, skipping rope and lifting weights, finishing off with a few rounds of sparring with his trainer, Martin Denny.

The fight was delayed until January 25, 1902, but was enthusiastically attended regardless. From the start, it was completely different from Smith's previous feinting display. It was a battle of powerful equals who rushed at each other like fighting cocks thirsty for blood.

Jack Grant was the referee, a man well loved and sought after for his knowledge of the ring and his impartiality. He knew Billy Smith well enough to know that it was well within Smith's abilities to wreak destruction by means of painful and damaging fouls. Sure enough, after getting knocked about by Neil in the tenth round, Smith created a flurry of a scuffle wherein Neil ended up on the ropes doubled over with pain. Few, if any, spectators could tell what had just happened, but Jack Grant had seen. He stopped the match and awarded it to Neil on a foul.

Afterward, Smith was beside himself with indignant fury, declaring that he would fight Neil anytime, purse or no purse. Neil, on the other hand, was not hesitant to tell reporters that after he had started to trounce Smith, he was suddenly thrown into the ropes and simultaneously butted in the stomach by Smith's head while being given an agonizingly painful knee to the groin.

Billy Smith was one of those fellows whose ability to reason shuts down under pain and stress. Ordinarily, he would not kick someone in the groin, but he had gotten away with his lightning-fast fouls before, although they were often famously noticed.

An Astoria sportswriter had noted this back in 1896, during Smith's last visit to Astoria, Oregon. The fight was set for August 20 at the Louvre, the brand-new music hall saloon built by the entrepreneurial August Erickson. It was a match between Smith (then welterweight champion of the world) and Jim Ryan, the Australian middleweight champion, for a $1,000 purse. The article called it a "characteristic" match for Billy Smith in that it was filled with multiple fouls and should have been given to his opponent in the first round. Several times he was seen kneeing Ryan during a clinch—an act that brought hisses from the crowd. After the seventh foul-filled round, Jack Wilson, the referee, gave the match to Ryan. This sent Smith into a fury. He flew at Wilson, striking him in the face. Wilson came back swinging. By then, the police had intervened, and Smith was removed from the building while the spectators hissed like a pit full of serpents.[79]

## WHERE IS THE MONEY?

When everything is taken into consideration, prizefighting at the turn of the century did not pay well. Outside of a few large prizes, the profession was also fraught with expenses: train tickets, hotels, baggage costs, managers, promoters, girlfriends, police court judges—everyone, every movement costing money. Billy Smith hated to be broke. He was a champion, a world champion, so where was the money? Even John L. Sullivan himself had gone bankrupt at one point. Now he was proprietor of a cozy saloon in Boston called the Champion's Rest.

In Portland in 1903, there was an ex-pugilist of no real reputation (except having John L. Sullivan as godfather of his son). This would be the now middle-aged Larry Sullivan, portly, pompous and bloated with money, power and influence. He arrived at this position of wealth, including a fine mansion in Nob Hill, by robbing the lowest of the low—the poor sailor—of his clothing, provision and wages at the Sullivan, Grant Bros. & McCarron's Hotel for Sailors and Farmers on Second Street by the Steel Bridge.

## THE WHITE BROTHERS AND "MYSTERIOUS" BILLY GO CRIMPING

At some point in early 1903, Billy Smith joined forces with Harry and Jim White, two local ruffians who had been making a living working as runners for Sullivan's sailor's boardinghouse. Smith had made Larry Sullivan's acquaintance early on and through that connection met the two White brothers. After meeting over multiple pints of beer in a local saloon, it seemed that all they needed to go into competition was a place to house sailors now that they had an imposing prizefighter to cow the authorities, as Sullivan managed to do. Sometime before February 1903, the men rented a place in Albina at the foot of Russell Street, possibly thinking they could better get away with being in competition with Sullivan if they were across the river from his establishment. However, in those days, the huge grain warehouses, sawmills and flouring mill of Albina received the greater share of Portland's export commerce, a plum the Sullivan outfit was not about to share. The downtown docks were, by that time, all ferry docks and boathouses, and the north end warehouses were not as large as the ones across the Willamette in Albina. Following the death of Jim

Turk (the grandfather of shanghaiing in Portland), Larry Sullivan had consolidated the various sailor's boardinghouse establishments in Astoria and Portland. His company now exercised virtual control of the two ports, something that Sullivan would not see disrupted by a couple of turncoats and a nearly washed-up prizefighter.

With stool pigeons and police on Sullivan's side, trouble for the new sailor's hotel wasn't long in coming. Mid-February, soon after starting business, the two brothers and the boxer found themselves in the dock for kidnapping a sailor from the British grain schooner *Riversdale*. The captain of the *Riversdale* was tired of using greenhorns supplied by the sailor's boardinghouses, so he tried hiring sailors on his own to make up for the deserters. Smith and the Whites waylaid three men who were applying to be sailors. Two of them escaped. The third, a young man named Buren, was taken into the custody of the Albina shanghaiers, who spirited him away to their sailor's abode on Russell Street. Then, in an attempt to re-create a scenario the Whites had seen used in Astoria, they got a saloon full of lowlifes from lower Albina to go down to the *Riversdale* at Columbia dock to pelt it with projectiles while yelling threats and curses.

I think it is worth noting that the *Riversdale* had been here before, and it seems that Sullivan—knowing the captain would be trouble—stood back and let Smith and the Whites walk into a hornet's nest.

When Smith and the two White brothers heard that the police were on their way to the Russell Street house with a warrant, they took their ward—visibly drugged—aboard the trolley car for Vancouver, Washington. (In those days, there was trolley service across the Columbia River.) This meant the kidnapping was of an interstate nature and far more serious than just hiding a deserting sailor in an attic.

The three men were arrested, resulting in a flurry of graphic headlines and a protracted trial. By March, the district attorney had dropped the charges against Billy Smith and Harry White, for lack of evidence, after they had each pleaded guilty to a lesser offence and paid a $250 fine. Jim, however, continued to insist on his innocence and was convicted and sentenced to one year in the penitentiary—becoming one of the few people in the history of the state to be convicted for shanghaiing. In those days, a year in the Oregon State Penitentiary was like a year in the third level of Dante's *Inferno*. Jim White appealed and remained out of prison while on bail.

## JOE WALCOTT VERSUS "MYSTERIOUS" BILLY SMITH

Although the name "Mysterious" Billy Smith was always connected with the White brother's Albina house, it is likely that he was in training at the time of the *Riversdale* incident, making his participation seem minimal. It was a long shot for Smith to fight Joe Walcott again, the bout for which he was training at the time. Walcott was the man they called the "Barbados Demon," or just the "Demon." He could match Smith in ferocity and surpass him in "science." Smith had already waged battle with Walcott five times previously, winning only once, drawing twice and losing the last two bouts.

At this time in Smith's life, he had many distractions. He was at war with Larry Sullivan and others. He was battling the courts for crimes committed against sailors, and his new marriage to another very young woman was disintegrating rapidly and dramatically. He was unable to keep up a prizefighter regimen of diet, exercise and pugilistic training in the face of all this confusion. With the added setbacks of an unrestrained appetite for food, booze and girlfriends, Billy Smith did not stand a chance against the "Demon."

The match was held at the Exposition Building, under the banner of the Columbia Athletic Club. The evening of the match—a clear but breezy night at the end of May—there were dozens of uniformed police in attendance. The crowd showed up early and eager to be entertained, filling the floor seats and spilling into the balconies. When the fight began, it was with a flurry of fists and powerful blows. The first two rounds flew past with furious fighting from both men—and then suddenly, in the third round, there was an agonizing *snap!* as Billy Smith's left hand came down like a sledge hammer on Joe Walcott's head. From then on, Smith was unable to use this hand—a detail that did not escape the eye of Walcott. When Walcott realized that Billy Smith was still not using the hand in the fourth round, he came on him like a tiger on a cobra. By the end of the round, he had knocked the wind out of Smith and had put an end to Smith's desire for more punishment. The fight was suddenly over, a TKO (technical knockout) in favor of the gentleman from Barbados. A rather large irony is the fact that, just prior to the match, Smith had objected loudly to the bandages Walcott was wearing to protect his knuckles. Had Smith also worn bandages, rather than insisting that Walcott's bandages come off, he might have saved his own hand from injury, allowing him to win the match.

## THE MONOPOLY ON MARINERS

With Jim White in the penitentiary, Billy Smith and Harry White still thought there was room for them to make a fortune like the downtown sailor's boardinghouse. During this time, they were even dragged into court for threatening to kill Peter Grant because he had brandished a pistol at "Mysterious" Billy Smith (as his name is recorded in court records). Pete Grant complained in court that he had to carry a pistol because of Smith, and the pistol ruined the way his clothes fit, but he did mention that he would not hesitate to shoot Smith if he came after him, even in a courtroom. Since it was a police court, the judge had the leeway to tell the men to go their ways and act more mature in the future. This he did without even obtaining a promise of future good behavior.

The legislature of Oregon, in its great wisdom, created a Sailor's Boarding-House Commission to license sailor's boardinghouses and to take complaints from shippers or others with interest in maritime trade concerning the shipping of sailors out of Oregon. From the viewpoint of the Sailor's Boarding-House Commission, the port of Portland needed only one establishment for sailors—that of Sullivan, Grant Bros. & McCarron. Billy Smith and Harry White spent the money to fight this ruling all the way to the Supreme Court of Oregon. The ruling of the higher court backed up the authority of the commission, but not to create a monopoly, even if it believed that it was in the best interest of the port.

By this time, however, the monopoly was dissolving naturally. The downtown sailor's home was changing hands, being put in the charge of Jack Grant. Larry Sullivan and Peter Grant had read the writing on the wall. Portland politics was swinging to the "progressives." These were the women suffragettes, the prohibitionists and all the other people the folks in Portland's north end called "do-gooders." It seemed that any purveyors of vice were in for a long, dry season—few would have believed the severity of the coming "drought" or the length of the years that would be given over to teetotaling or bootlegging.

## THE TROUBLE WITH "MYSTERIOUS" BILLY'S WIFE

By the middle of 1905, Billy Smith and his second wife, Mary (known to all as "Mamie")—a woman he had married seven years earlier—started to threaten each other with divorce. It was the beginning of 1906 before the ball started rolling through the courts. Billy claimed that Mary was a drunk, and she claimed that Billy was unfaithful—even going so far as to name the woman with whom her husband was entangled, a Mrs. Josephine Burde, recently divorced in Oregon City.

By this time, Billy Smith had been set up in business at the Atlantic Café, at Third and Pine Streets, a saloon owned by Larry Sullivan. Sullivan was not one to bear a grudge against former competitors, often hiring them to work for him. Smith must have done other "jobs" during this period, for Sullivan and for others. According to his disgruntled wife, Mamie, Billy Smith helped Sullivan shanghai sailors. She put Smith's income at $500 per month, while he told the court he was lucky if it was $50.

## THE "COCKNEY KID," AKA "BARROOM LOAFER"

Another glimpse at underground (and unreported) income for Smith came to light in May 1906, when in the sleepy burg of Rainier, down the Columbia River toward Astoria, the editor and the assistant editor of an Anti-Saloon League paper published there were savagely beaten by a thug. The thug, when apprehended, turned out to be a young "barroom loafer" from Portland who called himself the "Cockney Kid." Without ferreting out his real name, the authorities put him in jail at Saint Helens to stand trial for the beating he had given two ministers of the "Gospel Against Booze." The Cockney Kid then blurted out his confession. The Rainer saloon owners had paid "Mysterious" Billy Smith to have the two gentlemen trounced. Smith, in turn, had hired the Cockney Kid. Although the story carries with it the aroma of truth, the district attorney of Columbia County never saw fit to follow the lead given by the kid.

## A PLATEFUL OF TROUBLES

The same day the story broke of the arrest of the Cockney Kid, Mysterious Billy Smith had his place of business, the Atlantic Café, shut down by the sheriff—impounded for nonpayment of support due to his ex-spouse, Mamie. The protest from Smith was strong and immediate. He was not the owner of the property, just the manager. He had nothing else for anyone. He was as broke as a vagrant, a hobo; how could he fulfill his wife's wishes for an extravagant life?

The only good thing to happen to Smith that year was when that great confessor the Cockney Kid wrote a lengthy (and rather amusing) letter to the editor of the *Oregonian* taking all the blame for the assault on the Anti-Saloon League men.

The once valuable intangible asset found in the good name of Mysterious Billy Smith was fast turning into mud in the Portland press. It must not have occurred to Smith that Portland had recently undergone massive change. The do-gooders were now running the show. Little peccadilloes, such as selling absinthe to a sixteen-year-old girl, or staying open past the closing hour of 1:00 a.m. or threatening to kill Jim and Harry White, were no longer business as usual.

## THE TROUBLE WITH JIM WHITE'S WIFE

By this time, Jim White's appeal had gone through the courts, and he had lost, which meant a year in torment. Governor Chamberlain—a sort of Robin Hood to the lower classes—stepped in at the last minute and offered him a pardon, provided he pay a $250 fine and court costs of $100 and keep his nose clean in the future. The governor claimed that the two guiltiest men got off with a fine, so prison for the least culpable was unfair.

When Jim White got out of the limelight, he went to work with his brother, Harry, and Jack Grant—briefly. His brush with prison left him awfully thirsty. He was probably flush with some guilt money from his brother when he became attached to a perky young prostitute, much to his wife's disapproval. Not being a woman to take things sitting down, she soon discovered her husband on Albina Street with his new girlfriend. She drew a pistol and fired four shots into his back.

White fell to the ground, crying out, "Oh! Oh! Oh! You've shot me!" His wife was then reported to have stood over his body with a resigned sort of look. "I only wish it had been me instead of you," she said. His strumpet friend was seen in several north end saloons that night, laughing about the shooting. She recalled that when Jim's wife showed up, "It was me to the woods!" meaning that she had made tracks as soon as the shooting started.

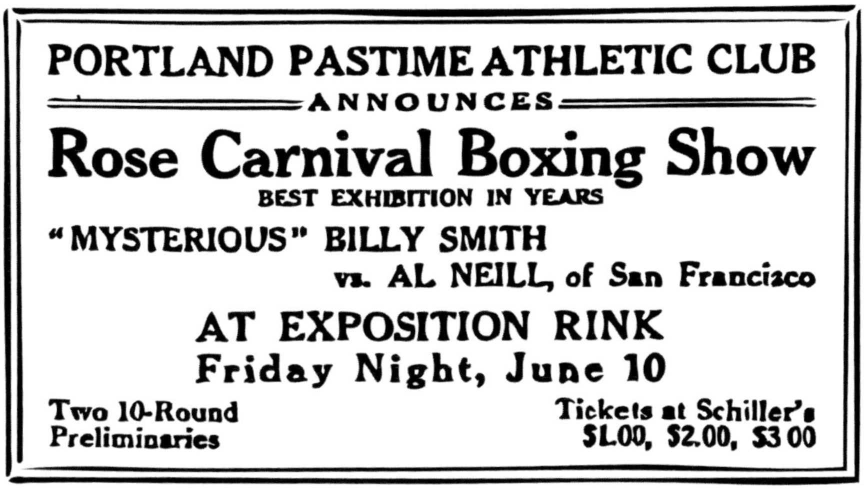


Rose Carnival boxing. *Facsimile of an advertisement in the* Morning Oregonian, *June 9, 1910.*

It was not expected that Mr. James White would recover. He was blind drunk when shot, and he claimed to have (miraculously) shot himself in the back. He later recovered, as did—presumably—his marriage.

## A Brief Stint at Bigamy and an Even Briefer Reoccurrence of Shanghaiing

It so happened that on June 7, 1907, Mrs. Mamie Smith was told by a judge that she was granted a divorce from Billy Smith. This fact must have reached the joyful ears of the pugilist, for the very next day he donned a tuxedo and headed for Oregon City, where he was wed to the aforementioned (by Mamie) Mrs. Josephine Burde. Known for jumping the gun in the ring, this amounted to jumping the gun with the ring. It seems the judge had told Mamie the divorce was final on Friday but had not signed the papers until Monday morning. In a society where divorce was frowned upon and remarriage was deeply frowned upon, marrying immediately upon divorce was in the worst possible taste, and bigamy was very, very bad indeed and very illegal. An average Portlander would not be able to show his face in public if he had received the onslaught of bad press Billy Smith received, but Billy Smith was not an average Portlander.

The incident resulted in a lot of self-righteous "harrumphing!" and very bad press, but little else.

During this period, it seemed Billy Smith was determined to see bad things written about him in the papers. The old phony of a blowhard shanghaier called Bunko Kelly got out of prison in 1907 after serving thirteen years for a murder charge he claimed Larry Sullivan had trumped up to get rid of him as a competitor. Billy had not been in Portland during the old days of Bunko Kelly, so he didn't know better than to stay away from a man who would rather tell stories about his exploits than actually perform any deeds of daring and lawbreaking. Bunko had somehow caught the ear of some big, dumb boys named Jost from the dry wheat lands of eastern Oregon. These boys had been punching on each other since they were babies, and now they wanted to get paid for the opportunity by becoming prizefighters. Bunko knew how they could make big money—even while they trained and looked for challenges. Another old-timer roped into the scheme was the aging prizefighter and bouncer known as "Jumbo Reilly." Naturally, they were all arrested for running a sailor's boardinghouse business without the proper licenses. The Jost boys were informed that they could never get a license if the names of Bunko Kelly, Billy Smith and Jumbo Reilly appeared anywhere on the application.

## PRIZEFIGHTS AT SAINT JOHNS AND SAN FRANCISCO

By 1910, it had been seven years since Billy Smith's battle with the Barbados Demon, and once again Billy Smith was ready for a comeback. According to the 1910 census, he was thirty-eight years of age; his wife, Josephine, was twenty-eight years old; her son from a previous marriage, Bernard, was eight years old; and the daughter that Billy doted on, Adelia or "Sazzy," was three. Billy may have become a jack-of-many-trades, but the profession he gave to the census worker was "pugilist." The rising progressive movement was not making it easy to be a pugilist in Portland. The new sheriff had a bad attitude toward the sport. No prizes could be awarded, the maximum length was ten rounds and there could be no blood and no knockouts. It was hardly the same sport.

The Portland athletic clubs would have nothing to do with a "Mysterious" Billy Smith comeback, but downriver in Saint Johns, the new Saint Johns Athletic Club, under the direction of "Professor" Ely, was willing to pit the local hero against someone big, or sort of big. By June 8, a Wednesday evening, it had a boxing lineup for the Saint Johns Skating Rink. It would be "Mysterious" Billy Smith versus Al Neil for ten rounds. Neil was a San Francisco fighter who had been on a losing streak since 1909. After losing that night to Billy Smith, Neil fought once more in Astoria and then threw in the towel and quit the sport.

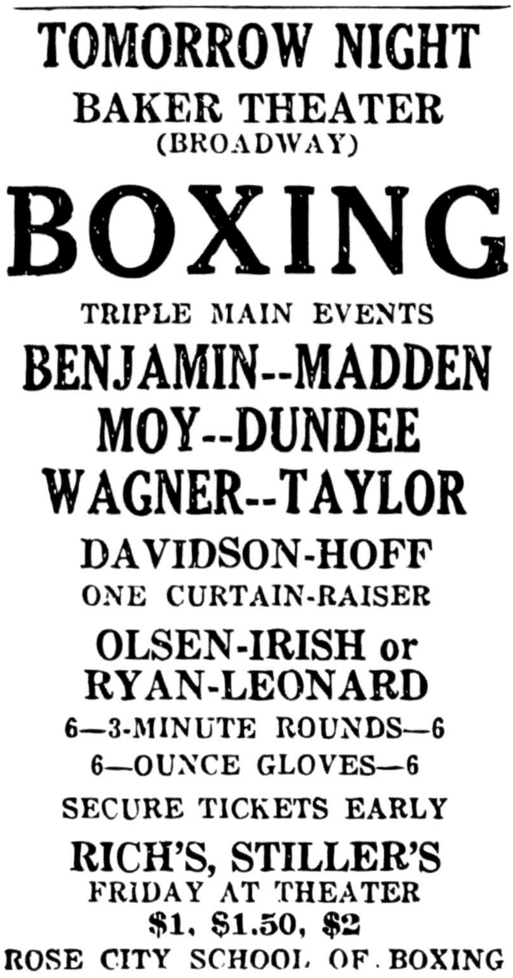


Fred T. Merrill's Rose City School of Boxing carried on with the new rules, using big gloves and short matches. *Facsimile of an advertisement in the* Morning Oregonian, *September 26, 1917.*

Billy used the win as a ticket to a bigger fish fry. Finally, a year later, he landed a fight in San Francisco against Rufus Williams at the Dreamland Skating Rink. Rufus chose to be ill rather than to fight Smith, who even after a year of training still carried an extra thirty-five pounds of flab on his welterweight frame. A substitute was found for Williams, someone more Billy's size, an up-and-coming heavyweight named Jim Cameron. When Cameron started landing hard punches, Billy lost it, reverting to his old-time dirty tricks. In the third round, after many warnings and fouls, Billy Smith forfeited the game for some of his old head-butting and groin-kicking moves. Under the heading: "'Mystery' There No More," the San Francisco sportswriter Harry D. Smith summed it up by saying, "Smith has no business in the game."

# TWISTED TALES OF WICKEDNESS AND VICE

It was a freaky year for the fighter who would soon be called the "freakiest pugilist of the age" by sportswriter Roscoe Fawcett in a premature obituary. The fact that Smith felt good after months of training made him begin to imagine that his former greatness was back. This boosted his narcissistic ego, making him crazier than usual.

For some years, Fred T. Merrill, the owner of Merrill Cyclery downtown and a boxing school and manager of the Rose City Club, owned a farm and an adjoining roadhouse twelve miles from the city on Base Line Road (now Southeast Stark Street). The saloon, called Twelve-Mile House,[80] was more like a nightclub, with an orchestra and dancing. It was the place for "fast" young people and was said to have rooms upstairs. Other attractions were auto races, horse races and cockfights. The building that held the saloon had been constructed in 1904 as the Telephone Building for the Lewis and Clark Fair the following year. It was adorned with neoclassical cherubim and other terra-cotta decorations, giving a sort of surreal effect to events held there.

Hearing of the success of this venture, in 1910 Billy Smith obtained a place seven miles from the city on that same arrow-straight boulevard, which he proceeded, cleverly, to name Seven-Mile House. This roadhouse was the sort of place to which preachers would refer as a "den of iniquity." The doors would open only to certain chauffeurs, the booze was unlicensed and clients were sometimes kept long beyond their desired stay so money could be milked from them. The chauffeurs would cruise downtown looking for young girls to entice into "joyriding." The girls were bait for men with money to spend at a roadhouse. For many a young lass, this was the road to perdition.

In April 1911, the Seven-Mile House was raided by sheriff's deputies. Billy Smith and his wife, Josephine, were arrested and later convicted and fined for selling liquor to minors. For reasons unknown, this event caused a rift between the couple. Josephine divorced Billy and immediately married again—a small, proper sort of man named Albert B. Loomis, captain of the riverboat *Weown*. The marriage was a step up for Josephine—especially after the indignation of her arrest. Billy Smith was still crazy about her, and he was even crazier about his cute little five-year-old, "Razzie Raspberry." He stalked Josephine. He purposefully ran into Captain Loomis. If you recall, Billy Smith was a welterweight, yet he towered over Loomis, causing his ruddy freckles to pale and the short, red stalks of his hair to stand on end. Billy Smith used foul language and threatened to kill Loomis "like the dirty dog that you are." Following this encounter, Loomis paid a visit to a gun shop, purchasing a Colt M1900 self-loading semiautomatic .38-caliber handgun. Smith, on the other hand, carried his .45-caliber Colt single-action army revolver. It was like the Wild West, a gunfight waiting to happen.

Mr. Loomis may have seemed a proper gent in his conservative suit, with his gentle, mollifying manners and earnest eyes bulging behind his spectacles, but he was mad about Josephine, whose animal pheromones had caused him to lose all notions of propriety in a green haze of sexual jealousy. He had seen his wife and Smith together before—even though she had sworn off the pomp and glory of that pugilistic devil and all his works. It was about nine o'clock on the evening of December 17 when Billy Smith and his ex-wife met at the Levin Café on Pine Street in what seemed, to the eye of an observer, to be a clandestine tryst. That observer happened to be Captain Loomis, who came up quickly with his pistol drawn from his overcoat soon after the couple left the café and was walking down Third Street. Josephine saw her husband and grabbed Billy, yelling, "Look out!" but by then two bullets had ripped into Billy's abdomen. As Billy Smith groped in his coat for his Colt, one more bullet ripped into him. As Loomis ran off for the alleys close to the waterfront, Billy's Colt did manage to ruffle the redhead's feathers, one grazing him under the arm and the other blowing off a piece of his coat.

With blood oozing all over him, Billy laughed off the hospital, claiming that a pharmacy could fix him up just as well. He was helped into the nearby pharmacy at Third and Burnside Streets, where he fainted away from loss of blood. He was taken by ambulance to Saint Vincent's Hospital at the top of Nob Hill. Having awakened in the ambulance, Smith refused the stretcher, walking unsteadily to the elevator, where he collapsed once more. He awoke once more outside the surgery door while doctors prepared to operate to remove the bullets. His former wife was with him, and he held his precious little five-year-old "Raspberry" in his arms. A man from the district attorney's office was there to take his statement, telling Smith in no uncertain terms that this was his deathbed statement and would carry great weight because of it. Smith laughed and told little Raspberry not to worry, that he wasn't about to die anytime soon.

## THE PREMATURE OBITUARY

Around the country, newspaper editors, weary of cheerful Christmas stories, printed long, eulogizing recollections of the life and career of "Mysterious" Billy Smith. It was great story material; every retired slugger had some tale to tell of the famous faker and fouler. Then there was the juicy gossip of little Albert B. Loomis, who had rushed off over the river on the Morrison Bridge and then turned himself in at the East Precinct with a lame lie: "'Mysterious' Billy Smith took a shot at me tonight and I was forced to shoot him. Have I hurt him badly?" The little man was immediately arrested on the charge of "assault to kill" and sent to jail to await the death of his quarry. By the year's end, the doctors announced that the danger had passed by and Billy Smith would likely recover. Once Smith was seen to be on the road to recovery, the district attorney let A.B. Loomis and Billy Smith know that, in his view, they were both equally culpable, and he would not bring charges unless they were indicted by a grand jury.

For once, Billy Smith was right; the bullets and the subsequent blood poisoning did not kill him. Exactly four weeks later, "Mysterious" Billy was in a four-round bout for fun with Jack Durante of Oakland, California. Because of Smith's unhappy meeting with Captain Loomis, the "pugilistic community" threw him a benefit. The event was held at Fred T. Merrill's boxing school hall and had eight or ten other pugilists on the roster. Ticket purchasers were informed that the benefit was to "send Smith back to relatives in Maine."

## "MYSTERIOUS" BILLY SMITH RETIRES FROM THE FOUR-CORNERED RING

At the very end of December 1915, at the age of forty-five, "Mysterious" Billy Smith went back into the prize ring in a match against Jack Root, a Portland heavyweight.[81] There are many instances, told by numerous witnesses, illustrating that Mr. Smith had a monstrous temper on a hair trigger. He was reported to have beaten people up for no other reason than the color of their skin. It is quite likely that no one in Portland, or elsewhere, was willing to chance telling Billy Smith that something he had in his head was a bad idea.

Jack Root may very well have been one of Billy Smith's protégés; he had put on bouts with his students in the past. The witnesses to the fight all seem

Here is where Billy Smith lived with his fourth wife, Mae. After he died, the Champion's Rest was renamed Mysterious Billy Smith's Tavern (1500 North Wheeler Avenue). This is a press photo by Tom Delay of a murder at Mysterious Billy Smith's Tavern in 1954. The tavern was torn down for I-5 construction five years later. *Courtesy of Thomas Robinson.*

to agree that Root spent all of his time trying not to make Smith look like a total fool. It then occurred to Smith that age forty-five is a respectable time for a fighter to lay aside his weapons (or his gloves).

During the Prohibition era, he got in a couple of minor bootlegging scrapes for selling booze out of a soft drink stand he owned in lower Albina. He then moved to Tacoma, where he lived until 1920 managing a small hotel and Turkish bath. While in Washington, he married a woman named Mae with whom he had a daughter named Delta. After returning to Portland, he was able to run a respectable beer joint in Albina called the Champion's Rest. He was living with Mae above the tavern at the time of his death on October 18, 1937. He was buried the next day, following a small, private funeral at the chapel of Miller and Tracy.

*Afterword*

# Three Portland Champions for the Ages

## THE "MYSTERIOUS ONE"

The "Mysterious One," as the sports hacks liked to call him, outlived his right to a champion's sendoff. He couldn't really expect a ripe old age either, but sixty-six was pretty good for a half-crazy fighter who went 100 percent crazy when someone hit him. He was said in several places to have a son named Thomas, who became a fighter known (briefly) as "Young Mysterious Billy Smith." I discovered that this was his son Brendan, from his marriage to Josephine. He was a lad who had no aptitude for fighting and soon disappeared into the fog of forgotten history.

As long as people collect early boxing ephemera and recall the days of the London prize ring rules, bare knuckles, and cleats, the name of "Mysterious" Billy Smith will be remembered. Some sportswriters recalled how he would go visibly berserk upon facing an opponent. Like a Maori warrior, with wild eyes and animal growling, he would pounce on his foe, perfectly willing to go to whatever extreme necessary to bring his enemy to the mat. He was a master of dirty tricks and was said by some fighters to have several extra knees and elbows that he could use "accidently" or with his well-known lightning speed. He has been called the "dirtiest fighter that ever lived," a reputation that will follow him whenever the old warriors are remembered. Even so, when he died, few people in Portland recognized his name. He lies in a grave marked with only a simple metal marker.

# AFTERWORD

# THE LAST OF DEMPSEY

The fight with Bob Fitzsimmons came to be thought of as the "fight that killed Jack Dempsey," which seems a little strange to me today since Dempsey obviously succumbed to tuberculosis, which had been weakening him for some years. Dempsey was convinced that fight had killed him and saw his disease as only a sort of side-effect. For at least five years, he had been having spells of the disease, which was correctly diagnosed by doctors

Jack Dempsey memorial page. *Courtesy of Oregon Historical Society, 003625.*

Jack Dempsey at home with his girls. *From* Morning Oregonian *sketch, October 23, 1895.*

he encountered by chance. His choice of doctor was one who would not tell him he was dying of the same sickness that had killed his father but would dream up a fantasy ailment requiring a liberal treatment with whiskey.

The last chance encounter with a doctor was one who came to Dempsey's assistance as he traveled with his family back across the States for the last time. The doctor told a Seattle news reporter that Dempsey was dying of tuberculosis, and the report was picked up by the newswire. Dempsey was not only dying as he returned to Portland, but he was also broke. He and his wife and girls moved in with Maggie's parents in their big house on Grand Avenue. He was well loved by everyone in her family, with whom he, respectfully, never discussed his profession. He was so hesitant to advertise the fact that he was a prizefighter that his listing in the *Portland Directory* gave his profession as "commercial traveler."

In the Brady home, Dempsey went in and out of consciousness as the time of his departure drew near. He was visited often by Dr. Harry Lane and the numerous close friends he had in Portland. For the sympathetic readers, local newspapers printed long columns about the tragic scene at the Brady house. Then, on November 2, 1895, Jack Dempsey, the "Nonpareil," died.

Two days later, he was buried in one of the largest funerals of the period. Mourners lined the streets between the Brady's house and Saint Francis Church, where the congregation was estimated at 1,500 people. Then the Nonpareil was laid to rest at Calvary Cemetery, where his wife would join him a few years later. As a sad ending to this tragic love story, Maggie, too, had contracted the dread consumption.

## THE UPROAR STARTED BY A POETIC HACK

Rumors, which follow a prizefighter like flies follow a hobo, followed Jack beyond the grave. While Maggie was ill, the family delayed erecting a monument over the fallen hero. Prior to Maggie's death, the family was approached about allowing Dempsey's fans to erect a suitable monument, but they refused, thinking a tribute to a prizefighter on holy ground was something the church would not approve. It also seemed an unwanted intrusion into a very private matter.

The year following Maggie Dempsey's death—while the Brady family was preparing to erect a suitable stone for both Jack and Maggie—Portland lawyer M.J. McMahon, seeing the unmarked grave in the cemetery off the muddy, rut-filled Burnside Canyon Road, took it upon himself to write a sentimental bit of poesy. The poem, filled with inaccuracies, is a sort of tribute to the forgotten champion. Bad as it was, the poem took on a life of its own, becoming one of the most widely read poems of the period. It was reprinted in newspapers, magazines and anthologies of verse:

> *"Jack Dempsey's Grave"*
> *(Shorter version, as published in the book* Songs of the Cattle Trail and Cow Camp, *1919)*
>
> *That man of honor and of iron,*
> *That man of heart and steel,*
> *That man who far out-classed his class*
> *And made mankind to feel*
> *That Dempsey's name and Dempsey's fame*

*Should live in serried stone,*
*Is now at rest far in the West*
*In the wilds of Oregon.*

*Forgotten by ten thousand throats,*
*That thundered his acclaim—*
*Forgotten by his friends and foes*
*That cheered his very name;*
*Oblivion wraps his faded form,*
*But ages hence shall save*
*The memory of that Irish lad*
*That fills poor Dempsey's grave.*

*O Fame, why sleeps thy favored son*
*In wilds, in woods, in weeds?*
*And shall he ever thus sleep on—*
*Interred his valiant deeds?*
*'Tis strange New York should thus forget*
*Its "bravest of the brave,"*
*And in the wilds of Oregon*
*Unmarked, leave Dempsey's grave.*

Before this poem, members of the athletic club in Brooklyn sought to have Jack Dempsey's remains brought to a churchyard there, where a suitable monument to the great Nonpareil could be erected. When the archdiocese was approached, it gave the idea a big thumbs down—it seems the Roman Church indeed does not permit statues to prizefighters to be erected on church property.

People stopped talking about the "old" Jack Dempsey, as he was overshadowed by a man born the year he died. William Harrison Dempsey took the name to honor the memory of the Nonpareil. He became the "Manassa Mauler" and the first boxer to have a million-dollar gate. With the new twentieth-century media outlet of radio, and then television, the new Jack Dempsey fairly well wiped the collective memory clean of his old namesake. Today, no pilgrims come to meditate at the old Dempsey's resting place. The quiet family grave in the well-kept Catholic cemetery gives no indication of the amazing life of this almost forgotten man, a hero to millions, the Nonpareil.

# AFTERWORD

# "OUR DAVE" PORTLAND'S HEROIC FIRE CHIEF

Dave Campbell came into the eye of sportswriters with the news of the Dempsey-Campbell match at the mouth of the Lewis River. He set out—half-hearted it seems—with his new best friend Jack to become a champion. He saw the life of the pugilist in the great cities of New York, Chicago and San Francisco, yet he chose to go home and fight fires. He had been a volunteer firefighter since his arrival as a youth. He was very popular with the fire crews and was the captain of the hose and ladder races in competitions with other cities. Among his many talents was a one for juggling pins—an activity he was happy to perform at public functions for entertainment.

Campbell could be prevailed upon to fight, if the conditions were right. One of his more well-known fights was close to his last. His love of the sport had waned; he saw the changes happening nationally, and a once mysterious, exciting, even illegal act was becoming commonplace, watered down and uninteresting to him. But a local bully needed a lesson. Larry Sullivan had

Detail showing Dave Campbell with the Lewis and Clark Fair Fire Department. *From City of Portland Archives, A2005-001—AP/6079.*

become a big man with a three-piece suit and a solid gold watch. He was in the habit of pushing anyone smaller than him around, and he ran a sailor's boardinghouse. People called him "Shanghai Larry" and gave him far more respect than he deserved. From the time Campbell rose to prominence as a boxer, Sullivan had been giving him the stink eye. For reasons having to do with Sullivan's ego, he was itching for a fight and making grandiose statements of his superiority to Campbell at every opportunity.

Finally, in late December 1890, the match took place at the Mechanic's Pavilion, with the watchful eye of the police at the proceedings. There may have been fools who put money on the pro shanghaiier, but he was no match for the gargantuan fireman. Campbell plugged Larry Sullivan hard enough in round four to put him on his back "listening to the birdies," as they used to say.

This was his ninth and last public prizefight, two of which he lost: one to Bobby Dobbs and the other to Jack Dempsey. Before Sullivan, he fought the great James J. Corbett, ex-heavyweight champion, to a draw. As a pugilist, he was of as good a quality as any man alive—but in his spirit, he was far more of a family man and community leader than a boxer. He was a natural figurehead to whom Portlanders referred as "Our Dave." When he led the fire department, he became known as one of the nation's foremost fire chiefs.

Dave Campbell's funeral procession. *Courtesy of Oregon Historical Society, 004494.*

A leader of men and head and shoulders above most men, not only was he asked to head up the Rose Carnival in Portland, but his towering good looks were required in other cities as well. In many ways, he was more the "face of Portland" to the world than any other person of his time period.

In late November 1901, the already popular fire chief married Miss Wiebe Scherener in a magnificent wedding at Calvary Presbyterian Church. He was living a far better and happier life than if he had chosen to take up fists as his profession. When Campbell perished in a fire in 1911 at the Union Oil Company in east Portland, Wiebe joined the nation's many fire widows. Following the funeral—held at the Elks lodge before seven hundred brother Elks—the procession moved through streets lined with tens of thousands of moist-eyed mourners. It is possible that Portland has never seen anything to match such a send-off. It was a funeral fit for an American president, and Campbell was in a position he had been in many times before—leading the parade.

## A FEW GRAVE MATTERS

Chief Dave Campbell. *Courtesy of Oregon Historical Society, 007911.*

In this book, I managed to discover a number of long-forgotten details. "Mysterious" Billy Smith's first wife, Minnie, was a Portland girl, the daughter of a carpenter. They were married during his first visit in 1892 in a private wedding. Following her tragic death from food poisoning in a hotel in Massachusetts a few months later, the devastated Billy Smith had her remains shipped back to Portland, where she is buried in the prestigious Riverview

Dave Campbell, the memorial at Eighteenth and West Burnside. *Photograph by author.*

Cemetery beneath a lavish and ornate monument that must have cost Billy the price of a house. The monument is lovely—a human-sized angel standing on a granite block inscribed with a plaintive poem about seeing "one's treasure" in the hereafter. It is on the opening page of the cemetery's website but without reference to who "Wm. A. Smith (husband)" may have been. Billy

Smith, however, is buried in a poorer, eastside cemetery, beneath a small metal marker that reads, "Wm A Smith." The marker was hidden beneath the sod for decades until someone recently went looking for it with a shovel.

Dave Campbell sleeps in Riverview with the city fathers. His monument, in the Fire Fighters Park on Southwest Eighteenth and Burnside, goes unnoticed by the passing traffic. There is serious talk about tearing down this unique and beautiful structure, assuaging guilt by naming a new fireboat house after the hero.

Jack and Maggie Dempsey lie in perpetual matrimony on Mount Calvary, sharing a stone that was erected sometime after Maggie's death in 1898. After all the hoodoo and hullabaloo over Dempsey's grave, no one noticed that the monument scribe put the date of his death as 1896 instead of 1895, adding a weird twist of irony as an end note to what seems to me a tragic love story.

# JACK DEMPSEY'S GRAVE.

---

Far out in the wilds of Oregon
On a lonely mountain side,
Where Columbia's mighty waters
Roll down to the Ocean tide;
Where the giant fir and cedar
Are imaged in the wave
O'ergrown with ferns and lichens
I found poor Dempsey's grave.

I found no marble monolith,
No broken shaft nor stone,
Recording sixty victories,
This vanquished victor won;
No rose, no shamrock could I find,
No mortal here to tell
Where sleeps in this forsaken spot
The immortal nonpareil.

A winding, wooded canyon road
That mortals seldom tread,
Leads up this lonely mountain
To this desert of the dead.
And the western sun was sinking
In Pacific's golden wave;
And these solemn pines kept watching
Over poor Jack Dempsey's grave.

Forgotten by ten thousand throats
That thundered his acclaim—
Forgotten by his friends and foes
Who cheered his very name.
Obliv on wraps his faded form
But ages hence shall save
The memory of that Irish lad
That fills poor Dempsey's grave.

Oh, Fame, why sleeps thy favored son
In wilds, in woods, in weeds,
And shall he ever thus sleep on
Interred his valiant deeds?
'Tis strange New York should thus forget
Its "bravest of the brave"
And in the wilds of Oregon
Unmarked, leave Dempsey's Grave.

—MAC MAHON.

Portland, Or., 1899.

Jack Dempsey's grave. *Self-published by Mac Mahon in 1899.*

# Notes

## Chapter 1

1. *Monday Oregonian*, "A Genuine Prize Fight," October 16, 1883.
2. *Morning Oregonian*, Advertisement, April 11, 1883.
3. "Shied his castor into the ring" is a nineteenth-century American slang phrase. (A castor is a hat; the word *castor* is derived from the Latin name for beaver, from whose fur top hats were formerly made.) James Maitland, *The American Slang Dictionary* (Chicago: R.J. Kitteredge & Co., 1891).
4. *Morning Oregonian*, "A Genuine Prize Fight," October 16, 1883.
5. *Morning Oregonian*, "Prize Fight Aftermath," October 17, 1883.

## Chapter 2

6. *Morning Oregonian*, "Not Knocked Out," November 8, 1893.
7. *St. Paul Daily Globe*, "Throws in Sponge," September 15, 1884.
8. *Daily Astorian*, "John Longfellow Sullivan," February 1, 1884.
9. *Morning Oregonian*, "Sullivan's Victim," February 2, 1884.
10. *Morning Oregonian*, "He's Here," February 4, 1884.
11. *Morning Oregonian*, "Won His First Fight," June 23, 1884.
12. The hotel mentioned is the partially built, long-incomplete Portland Hotel, a project of Henry Villard, president of the Northern Pacific Railroad. The bridge is the long-promised, partially completed, long-

overdue Morrison Bridge. At this date, the Columbia River Bar was still a great impediment to navigation, sometimes holding up ships for weeks at a time in bad weather.

## CHAPTER 3

13. For the full story on "Shanghai" Larry Sullivan, see Barney Blalock, *The Oregon Shanghaiers: Columbia River Crimping from Astoria to Portland* (Charleston, SC: The History Press, 2014).
14. Records of the Clark County Commission, Book C, November 28, 1885, 128.
15. This is in Cowlitz County, a place along what is today Dike Road at approximately where it is met by Whalen Road.
16. *Daily Astorian*, "Sullivan No. 2," September 13, 1885.

## CHAPTER 4

17. "Bagnio" was a common nineteenth-century term for a high-class prostitute's boudoir.
18. To avoid confusion, the "Nonpareil" Jack Dempsey was a fighter of the nineteenth century. The man born in 1895 who was a famous heavyweight champion during the twentieth century took the name "Jack Dempsey" to honor the memory of the earlier prizefighter.
19. Oddly enough, this cooperage shop at the same time employed Jack McAuliffe and Jack Shelly. Both of these men would also become world-champion pugilists in their own time. Sam McGinnis, "Slack Barrel Coopers," *Coopers International Journal* 21 (December 1911).
20. A Celtic martial art; Irish scuffling (Irish: *Caraoicht coiler agus uile*).
21. Richard Barry, "Jack Dempsey the Nonpareil," *Pearson's Magazine* 29, no. 4 (April 1913).
22. Ibid.
23. Some sources show this match to have been won in twenty-one rounds.
24. Richard K. Fox, *Life and Battles of Jack Dempsey: A Complete History of all the Battles Fought by the NonPareil Graphically Told and Handsomely Illustrated* (New York: Richard K. Fox Publisher, 1889).
25. Ibid.
26. Dialogue from Fox, *Life and Battles of Jack Dempsey*.
27. *Morning Oregonian*, "Suppress the Prize Fight," November 2, 1885.

28. Fox, *Life and Battles of Jack Dempsey*.
29. *Morning Oregonian*, "The Fight," November 3, 1885.

## CHAPTER 5

30. Much of this chapter is based on several newspaper reports, including, *Morning Oregonian*, "The Prize Ring," November 3, 1885.
31. Fox, *The Life and Battles of Jack Dempsey*.
32. *Morning Oregonian*, "World's Champions Once—Forgotten Now," July 3, 1910.
33. Richard Barry, "Jack Dempsey—The Nonpareil," *Pearson's Magazine*, April 1912.

## CHAPTER 6

34. *Daily Astorian*, November 6, 1884.
35. *Chicago News*, "Bill Nye on Pugilism," April 19, 1886.
36. *New York Sun*, "Dempsey Looking for a Fight," January 15, 1886.
37. Different newspapers state differing figures and details. For my information, I relied on the report of the *New York Sun* issue of February 4, 1886, and the Richard K. Fox book, which seems the most informed.
38. *New York Sun*, "Dempsey Gets the Fight," February 25, 1886.
39. Ibid.
40. Ibid.
41. Ibid.
42. Ibid.
43. *Indiana Statesman*, "Greatest on Record," March 17, 1886.
44. Ibid.
45. "Jack Dempsey," as repeated in the *Maysville Evening Bulletin*, July 22, 1886.
46. *Sacramento Daily Record*, "Dempsey Defiant," June 27, 1886.

## CHAPTER 8

47. *Sun*, "A Famous Fighter's Gloves," January 6. 1887.
48. Mike Donovan, *The Roosevelt That I Know: Ten Years of Boxing with the President—and Other Memories of Famous Fighting Men* (New York: B.W. Dodge & Company, 1909).

49. *Los Angeles Daily Herald*, "Dempsey and Donovan Fight Six Rounds," November 16, 1888.
50. *World*, "Sports, Track and Ring," January 8. 1888.
51. *Daily Morning Astorian*, "Telegraphic," August 25, 1889.
52. *Morning Oregonian*, "How La Blanche Beat Nonpareil," July 26, 1935.
53. *Morning Oregonian*, "Hazen Talks to Old Boxer," March 19, 1934.
54. *Morning Oregonian*, "Dempsey Wept," August 29, 1889.
55. The name given to the Australian criminals invading San Francisco during the gold rush years, giving rise to the Committee of Vigilance and a number of lynchings.
56. In actuality, Fitzsimmons's career was launched in Australia, but he was born in England, immigrating to New Zealand with his family while he was very young.
57. *Daily Morning Astorian*, "Among the Pugilists," October 12, 1890.
58. *World*, "Jack's Day Is Over," Extra Edition, January 15, 1891.
59. *World*, "John L. Is Plunged into Grief," January 15, 1891.

## CHAPTER 9

60. *Herald*, "Jack Dempsey Interviewed," November 14, 1891.
61. *Dallas Times Mountaineer*, "Astoria Talk," October 31, 1891.
62. *Morning Oregonian*, "Professor Dempsey—the Nonpareil Settles Down," February 14, 1892.
63. *Morning Call*, "Club at Portland," March 23, 1892.
64. *Morning Oregonian*, "Preliminary Bout," May 26, 1892. Note: In many boxing record lists, "Mysterious" Billy Smith is shown as fighting this battle on April 26, 1892. If Smith fought at the club on that date, he is not listed by name but falls into the "and others" category. The match with West is correct as I have stated it.
65. *Morning Oregonian*, "Smith Beat Maber Twenty-Six Rushing Rounds," September 21, 1892.
66. William Shakespeare, *Henry V*, Act 3, Scene 1.
67. Harry Lane was a medical doctor; U.S. senator; mayor of Portland, Oregon; and grandson of the original territorial governor of Oregon.
68. *Herald*, "Pugilists Past and Present," February 5, 1893.
69. *Evening World*, "No News of Jack Dempsey," June 14, 1893.
70. *Herald*, "Theatrical Matters," November 5, 1893.
71. *Washington Bee*, "This Week's News," November 11, 1893.

72. *North Platte Tribune*, "Worthy of Confidence," February 28, 1894.
73. *St. Paul Daily Globe*, "Dempsey Is in Fine Shape," December 14, 1894.
74. *Evening World*, "Dempsey's Shadow," January 19, 1895.

## CHAPTER 10

75. Genealogists, by unfathomable persistence, have ferreted out the information that "Billy" Smith was born Amos Smith, in Little River, New Brunswick, the son of a Scotch Baptist fisherman.
76. See *On the Waterfront*, directed by Elia Kazan.
77. *Morning Oregonian*, "Sporting," April 10, 1892.
78. *Sunday Oregonian*, "New Amusement Enterprise," July 2, 1893.
79. *Morning Astorian*, "Ryan Wins in Seven Rounds," September 4, 1896.
80. *Oregonian*, "Fire Wipes Out 12 Mile Tavern," May 19, 1939. The twelve-mile marker was at what now would be 217 and Southeast Stark. The tavern was moved there in 1906 and burned in 1939.
81. This was not the light-heavyweight champ by the same name who fought his last prizefight in 1906.

# Index


## A

*A.A. McCully* 54, 59, 61
*Ancon* 57
Astoria Athletic Association 85
Astoria Athletic Club 87
Atlantic Café 127

## B

Barbados Demon. *See* Walcott, Joe
Bixamos, Charley 49
Bogan, Charles 103
Bogue, Tom 66, 70, 73
Bourne, Senator Jonathan 54
Bowen, Andy 113, 116
Brady, James F. 64
Brady, Maggie 64, 78, 88
Burde, Josephine 127, 129
Burge, Dick 110
Burke, Ed 103
Burke, Jack 79

## C

*Calliope* 54
Calvary Presbyterian 144
Campbell, Dave 45, 51, 56, 63, 66, 144
Cardiff, Pasty 103
Carroll, Jimmy 67
Carr, Jim 49
Carroll, Captain James 57
Carr, Pat 80
Chambers, Arthur 67, 68
Champion's Rest 119
Choyinski, Joe 114
*City of Salem* 54, 59, 61
*City of Sellwood* 54
*Clara Parker* 56
Cleary, Tom 49, 58, 65, 68, 72, 73, 80
Clough, L.B. 39
Cockney Kid 127
*Columbia* 98
Columbia Athletic Club 125
Corbett, James J. 51, 92, 111, 143
Costello, Martin "Buffalo" 80
Costigan, Denny 90, 111, 112
Coyle, Jim 80
Cyclorama 105

## D

Dacey, Bill 88
Davies, "Parson" 115
Davis, Charles E. 81

Day, Jack 107
Dee, Matthew Mark 59, 84, 87
Dempsey, Jack "Nonpareil" 56, 82, 116, 141
Dempsey, Mike 88
Dempsey, William Harrison 141
Diamond Belt 75
Donovan, "Professor" Mike 88, 90
Dowd, Jack 26
Durante, Jack 134
Dyer, James 85

**E**

Ely, "Professor" 130

**F**

Fancy, the 13
Fawcett, Roscoe 132
Ferns, Rube 120
Fitzgerald, B. 57
Fitzsimmons, Bob 97, 138
Fleetwood 34, 54
Fogerty, Jack 69
Fulljames, George 48

**G**

Geer, T.T. (Oregon state senator) 63
Georghan, James 57
Gleason, Charles 103
glove contest 33. *See* Queensberry rules
Grant, Bridget 84, 86
Grant, Jack 86, 107, 122
Grant, Peter 107, 126
Gregory, L.H. 117
Griffin, Henry 25
Growriff, Sylvester 34

**H**

Hall, Charles 103
Herget, John L. 92, 98, 100
Hill, Barry 70
*Hudson* 114
Hyer, Tom 15

**J**

*Jabez Howes* 85
Jackson, Peter 115
Johnson, Albert 85
Jones, Harry 103
Jones, John 26

**K**

Keegan, Jim 70
Keenan, Jack 49, 58
Kelly, Bunko 130
Kough, Billy 103

**L**

LaBlanche, George 67, 70, 75, 94
Lane, Dr. Harry 107, 116, 139
Lavigne, George 103, 113, 119
Lawler, Pete 35
Leonard, Martin 85
Lewis, Bob 26
Lily, Christopher 15
London city rules 17
Loomis, Albert B. 132, 133, 134
Lucea Mason 39, 41

**M**

Maber, Billy 107, 119
Madden, Billy 90
Manassa Mauler. *See* Dempsey, William Harrison
Manning, Billy 50
Manning, Thomas 23, 30, 36
Mathews, Matty 120
McAulliffe, Jack 96
McCarron, Dick 58, 84
McCarron, Jim 85
McCarthy, Billy 113
McCoy, Pete 70, 71
McCoy, Thomas 15
McDonald, Duncan 38, 41, 58
McDonald, Ed 46, 47
McMahon, M.J. 140
Mechanic's Pavilion 35, 143

Merrill, Fred T. 132, 134
Mitchell, Charley 79
Morgan, Billy 23, 26, 33
Mount, J.K. 26
Multnomah Club 102

**N**

Needham, Danny 120
Neil, Al 121, 122, 131
*New York* 54
Nye, Edgar W. "Bill" 65

**O**

*Ocean Queen* 72, 73
O'Neil, Jack 36

**P**

Parrish, Samuel B. 35
Pastime Club 105, 121
Portland Cyclorama Company 101
Powers, Pat 104

**Q**

Queensberry rules 17, 33

**R**

Reagan, Johnny 88
Reilly, J.E. "Jumbo" 35, 42, 130
*Riversdale* 124, 125
Rodda, Jim 49
Roosevelt, President Theodore 17
Root, Jack 134
Rose Carnival 144
Ryan, Jim 122
Ryan, Paddy 33
Ryan, Tommy 113, 114, 115

**S**

Sailor's Boarding-House Commission 126
Saint Francis Catholic Church 64, 77, 140
Saint Johns Athletic Club 130
*Salem* 39
San Francisco Committee of Vigilance 15
Scherener, Wiebe 144
Schroder, Charles 50
Seven-Mile House 132
Sharp, George 26
Sheppard, Patsey 73
Smith, Al 35, 68
Smith, Harry D. 131
Smith, Mary "Mamie" 126
Smith, Minnie 109
Smith, "Mysterious" Billy 103, 107, 110, 135, 137
Smith, Paddy 103
Smith, R.S. 104
SS *Oregon* 34
Stevens, George 41
Strechan, F.W. 31, 35
Sullivan, Grant Brothers, and McCarron 126
Sullivan, John L. 17, 35, 41, 51, 66, 67, 90, 97
Sullivan, Larry 39, 59, 84, 85, 123, 124, 130, 142
Sydney Ducks 15, 94

**T**

Taylor, Charlie 80
Taylor, Joe 26, 35, 39, 41, 53
Thompson, R.R. 101
*Tilley E. Starbuck* 85
Tom Morris 39, 41
Tompkins, Dave 26
Tracy, Tom 121
*Traveler* 23, 30
Turf Exchange Saloon 85
Turk, James 84, 85
Tuthill, Gus 66, 67, 72, 73, 108
Twelve-Mile House 132

**V**

Verhaag, Father Louis 78

## W

Walcott, Joe 125, 130
Ward, Tom 59, 60, 84, 85
Warren, Thomas 85
*Weown* 132
West, Tommy 103
White, Harry 124, 126
White, Jim 124, 128
Williams, Rufus 131
Williams, Tom 120
Wilson, Jack 122

## Y

Young Mitchell. *See* Herget, John L.

# About the Author

Barney Blalock is a writer whose love of the Portland waterfront comes from the thirty-three years he spent working on the grain docks. His books, *Portland's Lost Waterfront* and *The Oregon Shanghaiers*, deal with the seedier side of Portland history. This exploration introduced him to the subject of this book: the bare-knuckles prizefights of late nineteenth-century Portland.

Barney is the great-grandson of Oregon pioneers and as such has had a life-long interest in local history. In 2013, he hosted a series of lectures at different Multnomah County libraries describing the facts and fiction of the old shanghaiing days. In October 2013, Barney Blalock appeared as a guest speaker on Oregon Public Television's *Oregon Experience* in a program called "Portland Noir." He is a member of the Oregon Historical Society and the Oregon Maritime Museum.